T0101903

CARRION

CARRION

of myths, Ferris wheels, and sunburns

essays

ॐ

Wes Jamison

2021
Red Hen Press
Quill Prose
Award

🐓 Red Hen Press | *Pasadena, CA*

Carrion
Copyright © 2024 by Wes Jamison
All Rights Reserved

No part of this book may be used or reproduced in any manner whatsoever
without the prior written permission of both the publisher and the copyright
owner.

Book layout by Mark E. Cull

Library of Congress Cataloging-in-Publication Data

Names: Jamison, Wes, author.
Title: Carrion: essays / Wes Jamison.
Other titles: Carrion (Compilation)
Description: First edition. | Pasadena, CA: Red Hen Press, 2024.
Identifiers: LCCN 2023041912 (print) | LCCN 2023041913 (ebook) | ISBN
  9781636281162 (paperback) | ISBN 9781636281179 (ebook)
Subjects: LCGFT: Essays.
Classification: LCC PS3610.A49 C37 2024 (print) | LCC PS3610.A49 (ebook)
  | DDC 814/.6—dc23/eng/20231103
LC record available at https://lccn.loc.gov/2023041912
LC ebook record available at https://lccn.loc.gov/2023041913

The National Endowment for the Arts, the Los Angeles County Arts Com-
mission, the Ahmanson Foundation, the Dwight Stuart Youth Fund, the Max
Factor Family Foundation, the Pasadena Tournament of Roses Foundation,
the Pasadena Arts & Culture Commission and the City of Pasadena Cultural
Affairs Division, the City of Los Angeles Department of Cultural Affairs, the
Audrey & Sydney Irmas Charitable Foundation, the Meta & George Rosen-
berg Foundation, the Albert and Elaine Borchard Foundation, the Adams
Family Foundation, the Riordan Foundation, Amazon Literary Partnership,
the Sam Francis Foundation, and the Mara W. Breech Foundation partially
support Red Hen Press.

First Edition
Published by Red Hen Press
www.redhen.org

Acknowledgments

I'd like to thank the editors and readers of the following publications, in which individual essays appeared (sometimes in (very) different versions):

Cahoodaloodaling Magazine: "No-One Suspects Your Shoulderblades of Wings"; *Fifth Wednesday Journal*: "How Not to Drown"; *Gigantic Sequins*: "Mother"; *Gone Lawn*: "Eve"; and *Wilde Magazine*: "Carrion."

I'd also like to thank my MFA cohort, Sharon Ryan Burns, Ali Carpenter, Micah McCrary, Toni Nealie, Colleen O'Connor, Ryan Spooner, Jenn Tatum, and Tatiana Uhoch, who saw countless of these essays and their revisions long before this even became a project. Thank you for seeing this as and for shaping this into a project, for your support and your trust. Thank you, too, to the professors who taught me not only how to write but also the essay as a practice: Aviya Kushner, Shannon Lakanen, David Lazar, and, most importantly, Jenny Boully, who formally advised this as a thesis, who encouraged me and reminded me to "trust [my] writerly instincts." And, of course, thanks to Red Hen Press, T.S. Eliot, and Virginia Woolf. Thank you, my family, for seeing me, even when the camera did not.

Contents

CARRION

Let me then create you. (You have done as much for me.)

—Virginia Woolf

Carrion

I have been lying about the ravens since the beginning. I have said I see them all around me and that they follow me; but I do not, and they do not. In truth, two nights in a row, I noticed three or four of them perched outside my window. I took two reddened-night photos, intending to track them, to see if they remain in or return to the same position, posturing, location. I never compared them, and they never returned, but they remain indexed in the photos and by the white excrement covering the lower branches of that tree.

I am lying still. There are no ravens in the Midwest. What I see, what we see when we see large black birds that are not blackbirds or starlings are crows. I call them ravens, because I do not like the word *crow*; because I would prefer them to be *ravens*, to be literal, actual, real ravens. But they just aren't, no matter how much I wish or weep.

I do not see ravens—and we must simply accept that the name I give them and the entities themselves are not consubstantial, that words deform reality, no matter the word I use, that calling a thing *a thing* does not make it *a thing* at all but merely a thing that I call *a thing* that you may call anything else—I do not see ravens all around me, no, but I have noticed one atop what seems to be a lightning rod jutting from the Germanesque turret on the building almost catty-corner from mine, though the lack of significant height probably would indicate that it is, in fact, a weather vane. Regardless. I have noticed one in the large grassy lot I walk past on my way from the train. Once, I noticed one near the park next to my apartment carrying a Ziploc bag of Cheez-Its.

When I come upon them, my reaction is severe. Maybe three years ago, I stumbled upon one perched on a handrail: it was larger than any other I had seen, it didn't move, and it was so close that I could distinguish, for the first time, individual oily feathers—see through them to the calamus, the quill. It was prehistoric, aged in a way that pulls gums from teeth, cold in a way that tightens flesh around a hair follicle, distressed and malnourished in the way we all eventually become ribbed and essential. The implied violence, its proximity, its lack of perceivable alarm at my closeness immediately frightened me, frozen by the fact that I could have reached out and touched it.

The quills seemed pungent and so uncannily similar to the roots of teeth: I was twenty-one and had just experienced my first wisdom teeth pains. I had recently extracted from an X-ray that, despite developing for those twenty-one years, the roots of my teeth were not yet complete, still open at the ends. As they broke the gums, I could smell them, like rot, not because they were rotten but because they were newly exposed, just as I expect our viscera do, never before having witnessed all this nitrogen, oxygen, argon.

The pain forced itself along my entire jaw and ear and gums and tongue and eye, a sign, I was sure, that these could not comfortably coexist with the others. They need to be removed. (I have yet to undergo this procedure.) I don't want to. They are mine and always have been. Despite how common wisdom teeth removal is and despite how we all lose our first set of teeth, we are each born with these, our teeth, and to remove them—to rip or cut or break them out instead of letting our bodies naturally reject that which is no longer useful—is to no longer be our original, whole, complete selves. I have known my adult teeth longer than I have not known them: the first were so short-lived, growing in before memory began and falling out before I could grow attached. But I know these teeth. *This* is the version of my body I know.

You are your teeth, as I am mine, in part, and we use not only our hands and feet but also our legs, our abdomen, our back, lungs, heart, brain, keratin, our carbon, our teeth to—whatever it is used for, the body is a tool. Newly missing teeth, our bodies are fragmented; the tool, perhaps, broken.

One interpretation would be that that raven forced an irruption of the Real (this is Lacan): the horror of it, the sudden realization that I am in need (constantly needing). Food, shelter, water, interpersonal contact, medication, transportation, hobby, occupation, money, limbs and digits, iron, to expel waste. We need these things—these things that are so apparent to others in our neonatal state—so that we may not die. Our entire existence, it seems, is based on needing not to die and to produce descendants; and children and animals, they are the ones whose lives of need are not censored.

But we cannot consciously live as they do: we cannot afford or are literally unable to tell each other, without that artifice of language, *I need to live*. When I write *I need to live*, I am just using the words to designate that which we designate as coming closest to the desired meaning, but that meaning is not the actual. Language cannot capture the semiotic, a mating call or the cry of an infant. Words are unable to capture, no matter how well-tempered they may be, the look of my grandfather's eyes when we found them still open and the oxygen machine still running and Animal Planet still playing when we found him dead. There is no eighty-one-year-old body with twenty minutes of decomposition already set in there.

I need to live.

All ravens have become symbol. I have found in all ravens that which I found in that first: I am growing, I am aging, I am dying, will die. And this growth, this progress, is painful. I will leave here neither whole nor unscathed. That pain—the pain I had to simply suffer through for weeks, that I could in no way curb or suppress, through which I simply had to cry, like this, and that fear, the fear of being attacked, of confronting something prehistoric and base: proof that we are mortal; our bodies, transient.

(This project is tricky, because I am circling the waters of the prelapsarian. But perhaps that's why I continue to write about these birds—only for the simple fact that I can't get it right, I haven't, and I won't. I will forever be *post*lapsarian, fallen, exiled from Eden, always cursed by the burden of language and its distortion.)

Words distort reality, and language is merely a fragile, so-breakable sheen over the body, bodies, the concept of *the body*. To say *I am dying* or *I feel like dying* or *I will die*—it means nothing. But the body can certainly *feel* or *know* or, in a way, *trust* that it will become inanimate, decompose, become something else to be used by something else. The body knows things we never can: for so long, I dreaded contracting HIV. The fear of complications (of the deaths caused by HIV) still persists, but the dread is gone: my body that wanted HIV got it.

The ejaculate stayed in me long enough for it to seep. My body created and then failed to close a bleeding open wound, accepting some number of viruses greater than twenty-five. They were attracted to it like a shark, and they couldn't all be killed by my defenses quickly enough.

I no longer *dread*, because it has already entered my blood and replicated itself through my white blood cells, ripping them from the inside out, leaving only these sheaths of procreation. I will certainly outlive any complications, but I grew up in a time when the most horrible thing about Matthew Shepard's death was that the officer who found him was exposed to HIV, a time when we were still being taught that just the diagnosis is a death sentence. That when that officer tested negative it was a relief. Regardless. No matter how much has changed since then, without medication, the body crumples in on itself from its lack of viable immune system.

Illness, *chronic* illness seems to be the only way to confront, accept, trust in our bodies' fleetingness. Only when we see our blood leave us in seven purple vials—and only when those are moved from our elbows to our own palms, holding our own heat. It seems to me that we can only know mortality if we are violently thrust into it, or if it is thrust into us.

And when our lungs or liver or knuckles or scapula or nerve

endings or sphincter are not suffering, or we do not know that we are, the ravens return to remind us.

My response to each and every raven proves they are more to me than just their bodies. Perhaps if I were ever in the mood to track and report on the purely physical, I would never have begun writing about them. But they are large and metaphysical, outside of temporality, inhabiting more than their own bodies.

I try to write the raven, the symbol and the body of the raven, but I cannot, because I have lapsed into language, and words only wrap themselves around and function as index to the actual. But to get to the truth, we have to confront the fear, our fears. Confrontation becomes easier when we deal with a physical manifestation or representation of something metaphysical. So I do not make much attempt at discovering what happens in a rotting body, a twenty-minute-dead body, but instead attempt to discover that which makes a raven not a crow and makes a raven fly and why a raven circles in flight and just how smart they are.

I write about ravens repeatedly, *knowing* that I cannot in this way come any closer to them. I never do: I never get any closer to approximating their bodies or that which they represent. Language is futile, because it is the body, not the language we use to describe a body, that holds meaning. But the attempts are not without meaning: I begin to circuit them, circle through currents of hot air, waiting to get high enough before I proceed, only to fall, then circle and rise again.

I want to outline them, provide silhouette, draw their perimeters, their limits; I want to wrap words around their mitochondria, their throat and crop, their crown, their mantle and flank, their secondaries and tertials, ribs and trachea, around their anterior-facing digits if no words may actually fill their void on this page. This is as close as I can come: if I may not *write* them, I'd like to *imply* them in this way.

Each time I circle, each time I prod at the corpse of a raven, I feel like I have found the heart of the matter, arrived at the center. To get past the first sentence, to leave that first sentence intact, we *must* trust that, if we are not there, at the center, we are at least one sentence closer. Of course, if the goal of writing is to confront that which frightens us, if we got there (where) in one sentence, we would be too scared to continue—always unable to say what it really was that we wanted.

Any word we write past the first admits that we are not yet there, though we are trying. If we could say it, could provide truths easily, clearly, we wouldn't need second, third, eighteenth sentences. We would not need books. (I would not need this book.) Art is predicated on the impossibility.

So, if we genuinely fear, we attempt and attempt again.

I write that they are following me, that I am special to them; but they are not, and I am not. Instead, after I write this, I convince myself of it, because I feel as though I have come as close as I can to the truth. These truths, preemptive.

I wanted them to think I am special. I wanted them to *need* me, to literally fall out of the sky without me. I wanted to be the object of their affection, their only and biggest carrion, their sun. But I am not. Not theirs. Even if they were temporarily mine, if I happen to be the one to notice their presence, I would merely be a short-term gallows-keeper, yet another hanged man to them. But I would be replaced. Yes, we all want to be the object of affection, but affection, desire, is discretionless, merely seeking placeholders. This is how desire functions: we do not desire X, we simply *desire*. Once we obtain X, we do not stop desiring, we find something else to desire. There are so many objects, states, statuses, stations we do not have, and, as long as we continue to *not* have them, it does not matter which we desire the most.

I need—I *desire*—to live.

It is not this simple. Were that accurate enough, four words would tell the whole of this truth.

I avoid the possibility that ravens could be just as meaningful to you. It's a messy idea. Symbols are cultural. Ravens mean only the exact same to me as they do for every other person who grew up or learned to understand them as manifestations of death, dying, disease. They are. Because they feed on carrion; because they spread bacteria and viruses; because they historically and mythically guard gallows; because they are black and black is, to a large population, representative of death; because their Latin calls warn us of *tomorrow, tomorrow,* and that is something we intellectually recognize we are not promised. For Westerners— those influenced by a probably singular worldview, probably spurred by stemming from a single cultural entity and further aggravated by a large, forceful theology—ravens are always fu- ture, blood, death, shadow, punishment, pestilence, illness, unmatched intelligence. But. I am particularly, unusually haunted by them. Because I allow myself to think that I am particularly, unusually aware of my body and my transience because I am constantly, daily reminded of it. Because my body contracted HIV. And I tell myself that this is because my body wanted to tell me that it will die—the virus, its language.

The three letters, that acronym is another symbol. For punishment, pestilence, sin, blood, death. For promiscuity, homosexuality, risk. Still. That it exists in my body and not solely in a collective unconscious makes me more aware of my mortality, my transience, of my death than others. Ravens are Jungian symbols, but I don't think HIV would be, since we do not often culturally encounter the actual image of it. But I wonder—and I cannot know—if we only recognize the raven's symbol once we are made aware of transience. That is, are ravens death and illness to me because they are to everyone or because I recognize my own.

This is what ravens become: the fact that you will soon die and that they will eat your tendons, ligaments, fascia, fat, synovial membranes, muscles, blood vessels.

I used to want to be cremated—have my body laid out for viewing and then pushed by my loved ones into two-thousand-degree fires where my body would crumble and split and char and break and continue to evaporate and oxidize and break and peel and divide and blacken until only close to five pounds of calcium and carbon remained. I used to want my ashes buried with the seed of a tree that would use some of my carbon to grow and produce fruit that would be consumed by animals that would release my nutrients by way of excrement elsewhere to be used by something else; or the fruit to drop to the earth and rot and be cannibalistically reused by the tree for nourishment.

I sought union with the Other so that I could live without language, without knowledge of good and evil, without banishment from the garden, without *without*; without being *dying* or only *HIV*, before simply existing. I wanted to live without questions or doubt. I wanted language to be subsumed by the body.

This desire to be prelapsarian is neurosis. (This is Freud.) I desired more than I do now a sense of eternity, a feeling of limitlessness, of being unbounded; I wanted to locate an oceanic feeling in myself; I wanted to float, be suspended and completely encapsulated, as if in the womb again. Cremation now seems to be a very clear attempt at climbing back into the womb by way of becoming one with everything. If I am separate from nothing, I cannot be separate from her, from you. All needs would be automatically met—there would be no *need*—because there is no resource, no object that is not already a part of me. I would, in fact, cease (to desire).

But I have reconsidered. I now desire an air burial: I want my corpse thrown onto the edge of a cliff, thrown onto a boulder and made vulnerable to the birds like Prometheus, except no healing, no chains, no fighting or screaming—just a dead body, just a stone, just the wind, and just the birds. Just carrion.

I am not sure how long my body would remain there on that stone, but eventually the birds, perhaps hungry and perhaps all at once, would remove my liver, my eyes, my veins, tongue and flesh. Everything soft would disappear into the maws of these birds while only my skeleton would stubbornly remain. The birds would consume me almost entirely and rise in warmth and fly over parched lands and defecate onto parched roots and foliage, transferring my basest energy—simple atoms—to them. I would become part of, used by, the birds and the plants and the fruit and the whole entirety of everything, eventually, just as I would be were I cremated and buried with seed.

But this is not why air burials exist: Tibetans are not deathly neurotic like the Judeo-Christian West. For them, there is no afterlife—only after life, only energy consumption. They are practical, scientific in this way. Air burials, unlike how I used to think of cremation, are in part about conservation of energy: nothing is to be wasted. Our carbon must not be boxed up and thrown into and separated from the earth; we must feed those who cannot easily find food. Our deaths are charity.

But it exists for another reason too. Death and decay and rot and whatever kills a person, and whatever feeds on that person in life or in death, is evil. And we must remain separate from it, lest we meet the same end. The stone is now evil. A corpse becomes evil, because death is evil, and things that feed on the dead, that use the dead, are evil; so if we touch it, we are too. We provide air burial so that our very society will not collapse in yellow smoke and plague, will not succumb to *evil*.

The problem here is obvious: I will die and you will die, and eventually each and every society *will* collapse. There is no avoiding this. So it is that either evil does not exist in this way, or we are always already in it: the body itself is *evil*.

Regardless, in an air burial, my anatomical, chemical, physical body would not be consumed by plant life or rodents or worms—I would be consumed by black hideous ancient dry birds that only feed on the dead.

So then this is what bodies become: food.

Dispose of my body however you wish. There is no loss of energy. Except in illness. That's how illness is defined: a loss of energy. Things, parts of us, decompose and separate from us. We lose our own energies. And this, I think, is the reason why I am writing any of this at all: it is difficult to believe that the body can differentiate between all the ways it can decay to only *thought* and *memory*.

Toxicity

I began with, *My chest hurts*. He began with, *Something to get off it*. I want to laugh now, because it is clever. But I don't. And I didn't. And, really, it is not.

He does not ask, *Who did you have over today* because he is innocently curious. Curiosity would lead to, *What did you do today*. Curiosity omits *who*. We ask, *Who did you have over today* or *Who were you with* or *Have you cheated on me* because we think the answer is *yes*. No matter the form they take, no matter their directness or candor or camouflage, the questions mean fear or worry or suspicion or, twice, accusation.

I would never. I showered, because I wanted to. I didn't feel my phone vibrate. Because.

My defensiveness about this is read as guilt. He cannot see how it would corrode and damage. (He cannot see that the innocent can be corroded or damaged.) He doesn't understand that chronic exposure causes irreversible side effects. And, really, how silly to need to explain why one takes a shower.

It pains me to think that you don't know me well enough to understand, to recognize that I couldn't. Love does not allow that to happen; don't you know I love you.

I began with, *My chest hurts*. He suggested I not smoke, but of course I have. That he said it made me want to smoke right then, because a part of me wanted to collapse and crumble and become completely unresponsive, to be found seven hours later. By him. That seemed the only way to prove how invasive and harmful the question was. My health, my body, and potentially his—because my body always relates to his body, it is part of our relationship, we are that kind of couple, apparently—is not as important as a thrashing suspicion. The problem is that, once relieved, another suspicion bubbles up in its place, and the more quickly you try to calm them, the more that arise and more quickly and bigger.

I have smoked several times already today. I think the manufactured mint of it has acted as an anesthetic or counterirritant. That is, the more I have smoked, the better I have felt. But then again, so often I *want* to collapse in ruin.

My pulse and breathing, both regular. Both fast, but normal. I went to the hospital once, panting and shaking and complaining of hurting and throbbing everywhere and how I couldn't breathe. The tests showed I was not lacking oxygen; I was breathing normally. I was told I could stop shaking whenever I felt like it.

Menthol is also a metabolic inhibitor for nicotine. It stays in my body longer, and I cannot process it as fast, and I continue to smoke, and I put more nicotine in my body that cannot be processed, and it is likely being processed more and more slowly as I am also exposed to more and more menthol.

There is something comforting, calming about the burn of smoking these mentholated, unfiltered cigarettes. Like intentionally flossing too hard, bleeding and scraping because I want.

I knew I had the desire to tell him when I first thought, *This feels like pneumonia.* I have never had pneumonia, and I don't know what it feels like, but I can imagine it. I don't know if I am imagining it correctly. Regardless. It feels like this.

But I can't have pneumonia, can I, since I have been vaccinated, by the insistence of my doctor. Because my immune system is impaired, and pneumonia is one of those infections that kills us when we can't fight it off.

I have explained HIV to him several times: it lowers your immune system until it is nothing, and without that immune system, you cannot fight off infection or disease. AIDS doesn't kill you. You die of a cold or pneumonia—those are the two that doctors mention most often. All the virus does is replicate. The body, a womb.

A friend said that we are suspicious of that for which we are guilty: I have tracked conversations with his ex. In one, *I love you.* He replied, *I will always love you.* In one, *I am pretty sure I have contracted.* He replied that to accept and understand is one thing, but one should not invite another foreign body into his life. But in none have I found anything suspicious, nothing to make me worry. Not any more than I do now, enough to follow these conversations. But I have yet to find *guilt*. And I don't think I will. Not because he is not guilty, but because he is too clever.

(Except this *is* his guilt. Except that, for so long, I've apparently been convinced one could love multiples simultaneously and differently; that residual, half-lifed emotions were normal and appropriate and did not get in the way of a relationship. How stupid of me, to see but not admit to the transgression. (Neither his nor my own.))

But I check because a friend suggested we are most suspicious when we are guilty. The more he suspects, the more I do. This is positive feedback, the beginning of a crumbling bridge. The way the wind wobbled Tacoma Narrows.

I began with, *My chest hurts*, but ideally, I would begin each of these conversations with, *I am not him*. I want to begin each of our conversations with, *Effective toxicity is determined by the relationship between the two parts*. I want to tell him, *No one thing is innately toxic*.

Periphery

I trust that his and my eyes are consubstantial. There is a filter, a glaze, a lens; there is something behind, inside, underneath. I feel it, this throbbing, this itch. Hyperawareness and self-consciousness.

And so I'm aware of where my gaze falls. Not of where I look, just of that which happens to be in my light of sight. Intentional, not.

I never wanted to be yellow. And yet, or perhaps *because*, so many of my memories are nearly all yellow: wheat, dry grass, book pages, hair, flesh, a little sand, soles of feet, light wood, autumn. For so long, I have desired gray, silver, metal, crowned, collared, opalescent-chested, white-tipped. But I've compromised: between bone-white and decomposition, between rust and moss, between cracked porcelain and October. I have chosen womb-life gray, a compromise between *imagined* and *experienced*.

This self-consciousness is not only of gaze but also of its consequence.

It is not the gaze that is the problem, but its intent. I don't want to be made responsible for what is uncontrollable. Because I want to say, *I can't help it* or *I look at a lot of things* or *It just happens that things come into my line of vision.*

This is not good enough.

A woman asked this child what color pigeons are. An absurd question. *Blue.* And he is not wrong. Add black to white to gray to green to pink to reflective chests of non-color—of course *blue.* Her face suggested surprise, and she said, *Yes, sometimes.* I wanted to scream, *No, you're wrong. Pigeons* are *blue.*

Someone walks by the room in which I sit. I look, because the figure is very tall, and I want to know *how* tall. I scratch my nose and look at my coffee cup, and I look away but back, because I notice the pink lettering as if it is new, but of course it is not. Another body passes by, and, upon looking, I recognize him. Thus, I am grateful I looked at all. (Why.)

While smoking, I looked across the street and examined a woman's coat, because it was very pink. I looked behind her, twice, because there was a man, and he was walking too slowly.

People pass this door, and I know because I see them in my periphery, but I do not direct my gaze away from the page. But I see them anyway. So I wonder if this counts, if that which is peripheral may be held against me.

I look at my coffee cup to see how much is left, because I thought to grab it, because I want to take a sip, but I look away and back at this page so I can coherently compose this catalog.

I looked at a man and a woman, because he was yelling loudly as they walked together down the sidewalk. I want to know why yelling, why sound, makes me look. Why I need to *see* to better *hear*, why things seem so confusing when heard but not yet seen.

I look at the power outlet, because it is framed by two windows with a metal-covered cord running to it from between the windows. There are two plugs in one square. I see it, and it looks so much like art, so intentional.

But we do not ask at what we look when we consider art. We only do when the intent of the artist is to direct attention at something particular. We only ask when we think there is something at which we should or could direct our gaze. *The* gaze. And only then when we find our gaze straying from that on which we are meant to focus.

Do we punish—are we punished for that which happens at the edge.

Rule of thirds. Line. Perspective.

I was rolling a cigarette, and I saw a bird on the ground, periphery, background. Because there is something about the eye that better allows us to focus on that which is in full sight. Depth perception and triangulation. I wanted to better locate it so I wouldn't crush it underfoot. Because I wanted to know what kind of bird. Because I wondered why I would look at a pigeon. Because I wondered why a pigeon would ever be so dark.

This morning, I was told I looked at a man coming onto the train. I don't recall looking at him. But I was told I did. I was apparently seen looking at a man coming onto the train. *This is the gaze.* I cannot say, *No*, but I can say, *I don't recall. It didn't register.*

To look: to direct one's eyes toward something to see.

To see: to perceive either mentally or with eyes.

I looked at him. I looked at lips and cheeks and eyes and eyebrows all almost simultaneously. One registered as sad, so I compared one feature to the rest: all sad.

So, perhaps, I saw him.

I looked between bodies, through the train window, at rooftops and birds and sky and power lines and trees graffiti cement subway walls and platforms. I struggled to look between bodies and toward the platform, because I wanted to see if his walk registered as sad too.

I lay my writing tablet down, and I look at its reflection in my phone. Because I could see the page's reflection in my phone.

Sometimes things are just this simple: just *because*.

I read what I have written, now, because I want to track the information. Because I have not gotten to the point. The point that the problem is that I supposedly look at men but maybe I don't or maybe I only see them and I don't know why. I don't think about why I see them or if I look at them, but he does and thinks he knows. The problem is that he sees a problem.

The point is that I think he thinks that I ought to be blinded or blindfolded when I am in public. So that he may not have this fear, this worry. Scoop out an eye and place it in a deep well.

For what.

As I wrote that, and now this, I looked closely at—I saw—the ink and how it is distributed across the page, thicker and wetter in some areas, and my gaze always lags behind the pen a little, because I want to watch the ink spread and dry, but I can't see the drying, because I have to keep up with the pen so that I can compose along the lines.

I see movement, and movement is seen, but one cannot look at movement. Objects are looked at, and sometimes seen. Temporality is not something one is able to look at. I am, then, always viewing twice, seeing simultaneously, double, like a hallucination.

I look at my writing, the purple ink at the top of the third page of this. It is when I said that I look closely at the ink and how it is distributed across the page. I see that the writing is so much clearer. I was closer to it, then. I had my head on my left hand, holding the left page down, my right dragging ink across paper.

There is no analogue here though: with proximity only comes distortion.

I do not know why I do not feel him inside behind covering, filtering my vision now. And I do not know why I am cataloging anymore. The point is made, I think—that whether I am looking or not, you are paranoid and accuse me regardless.

But I looked at leaves today.

I looked at leaves because they have changed since I last looked at them. I looked, because instead of being netted in the trees, they were strewn, now, under my feet.

I want to say that I looked at the lake in the morning, because I like to see the colors cast by the rising or seemingly always already risen sun. Because I like to imagine you seeing them, like to imagine that my eyes are in fact your eyes, and by looking, I am letting you see that on which my gaze is fixed. I want to know what you think when you see this line and these colors and the contrast—the black sides of buildings, painted that way, because the sun is still so eastward that it casts nothing on anything opposite yet. But there is so much reflection there over the lake that some mornings it is intolerable, and I don't know why we do not spend time there the way we once said we would.

Eyes have four and a half million cones, cells that turn light wave frequencies into electrical signals that are translated as red or as green or as blue. I know any three of the four and a half million can receive the same light wave and collectively determine any single color.

Compromise. (And how often does that mean *sacrifice*.)

Ninety million rods turn light wave frequencies into electrical signals that are translated, somehow, into sight, but not into color. I know they function in low light. Low light, less color.

I know that cones do not exist in the areas of our retinas responsible for peripheral vision. That is to say, our periphery is colorblind.

But I have seen *movement* in my periphery.

I look at his eyes out of the corner of my own. It is difficult, with glasses and no color, but his eyes are so dark and the whites are so white that the contrast makes them so obvious. I know where he is looking, and I know that he is so often watching me, but I don't know if he knows that I am actually watching him; and how often he is not looking at me at all but at other men. I think that he is looking at them because he thinks I am looking at them. Looking at them to determine whether or not I'd look at them, whether or not they are worth looking at; which, of course, means that he deems them worthy of looking at.

Something happens somewhere between the retina and occipital lobe. Solar energy, reflected how many times, is changed to chemical, to electrical. Color is only perceived, color is a process, color is something that happens, color is not tangible the way light waves are tangible, the way the sun is tangible, the way waves are tangible.

Thus, relative.

Carrion

Faceless. (I infer so much, so why not his, why not this. Because he has changed so much, perhaps, or perhaps because I know its irrelevance.) He was boarding or alighting the brown or the purple line train at Merchandise Mart. I see his black-Chucked feet, but not even these, just his pants, mostly movement. I see a flight of pigeons bobbing and treading around a dropped bag of chips, I see him see them and walk over to them, out of his way toward them—perhaps they were far off, not under the canopy by the stairs but out in the sun on the cement toward the front of the train—and steps on the chips. He steps on the chips so that they would become manageable, smaller, edible. For the pigeons.

I think it is possible that the restaurant at which he worked when he first moved to Chicago was off this stop. So often, I find that he has visited places, specific places we pass or that come up in conversation, and so often I imagine the visits are with or because of a boy. I attempt to convince myself that I wonder at this simply because he does not tell me; but, in reality, it is because I want to know what he has attempted to hide the most: his history, his life, his romantic life before me. I wonder, because I am jealous:

I said I wanted to see a burlesque show. How wonderfully exciting that would be. He danced, and I don't know how or can't or am not good, but I like to watch, and I would like to watch him, but we both like music, and we both like watching people dance, and we like that kind of music. How splendid. He told me, *Yes, we should,* and I was excited. He told me, *I have been to one once.* I asked *when* and *where* because I know he would not have gone alone and because I know he would not have answered the question *with whom.* That is, I asked *when* and *where,* because I wanted to know *with whom.* When he told me the place, the state, I knew *with whom,* and I immediately lost all desire to see a burlesque show. Because I do not want to repeat the recreationally romantic. I do not want to be part of a pattern. I think so often that I break them, but I hear things like this, and I wonder why he breaks the patterns for me, but I don't break his. Or if I do, then I fear so greatly being a pattern, being patterned, that I simply unconsciously convince myself that I do not.

I imagine that the pigeons parted like the sea for him. I imagine that he looked back to see what he had done. And I imagine that he was proud. It's there when he describes it, but only so much that *I* would notice it. Or perhaps it was never *pride* I sensed but excitement that he had done something that I find so special before we knew each other.

I do not know how many pigeons he fed that way. I imagine that there were a dozen in the flight, but a dozen would not have fit around a single bag of chips—maybe only a handful. But I imagine so many. Because pigeons are so often so many.

Even if a camera had been placed there, I would still have to imagine, as it could only capture movement and space and shape and contrast; I would still wonder about pride and intent and *from* and *to* and *whom.* I would need to hear his thoughts, loudly, to not have to compose them. I would need to see what he saw in order to not imagine that which he saw. To prevent imagining, pretending, I would need to *be* him.

These birds exist more fully and solidly than he does. I speculate so much about him, but pigeons are more fixed. And isn't *that* telling.

They are inquisitive, getting into everything: under banisters and inside electrical boxes on the sides of apartment buildings, huddled together on power lines and around bags of chips too large to be consumed. Their faces especially seem so, as their eyes are so stark and so open. And this is all so unlike all other corvids that the peculiarity seems all the more pertinent. Of *Corvidae*, the smallest are too small to think, to be anything other than toys for children or cats. The small ones are simply too small to be seen thinking, as all we can see of them is their entirety, not head movement or eyes. But the largest corvids— ravens and crows—are so smart; their intelligence and adaptation, unmatched. Their eyes, they are harder to locate and cannot be seen looking around, questioningly. Their brows are more forward, though not furrowed, larger, not as retracted and stupidly small as their family members'. Not only are they smart, but they look it. They are not inquisitive, as they already know.

It was a *particularly* intelligent bird that Noah sent first, but to send our brightest means to send our scavengers. Noah sent out a raven from his ark. Nothing on the ark was awake, and so nothing on the ark died, and so the raven was starving. Noah sent it out, and it did not come back. We can only infer that it finally found something to eat, the drowned and disinterred. This is the story with still-moist dead bodies and flesh-tearing that happens offstage.

But I prefer the version of the story where the raven wouldn't go, the version where the raven knew of Noah's cruelty, his responsibility, his role in the annihilation of species. This is the version of the story where the bird wanted the safety of the ark despite its fear of the man who lives there. So Noah sent another in its place, smaller and white. I like this version of the story, where Noah has two birds: black and white, first and second, good and *good enough*.

That dove isn't the symbol of hope we make it. That dove is a pigeon, because all doves are, because doves are just white pigeons, hated, flying rats. Homing birds, compass birds. Good enough, not as smart, but the iron in their beaks keeps them from getting lost. So maybe this means the raven died, mid-flight, falling into this swollen ocean, never reaching the land it was so desperate to find. Maybe the pigeon would have been a better choice for Noah from the start.

And I imagine homing pigeons being replaced by ravens to carry our messages through wars.

To Build a Ferris Wheel

I like to locate pain within his body. (No, not *pain*. I like to locate what wounds him from within his own body. (No. I like to *control* the pain experienced by his body.)) I want to control nerve endings and synaptic fires. (I want to control a body.)

I concentrate deeply, furrowing my brow as I start low and go up, pressing loose that which has become brittle and swollen and grown, and then I go down, circling and concentrating deeply and licking my lips and licking them again until they chap. I rub as if I am rubbing clean, creating that black eraser residue, that black rolled-up sheet of dirt under my thumbs. Something leaves him, I know, though I could never say what—I haven't figured that out yet.

(What is black in his body. What is the black that I am forcing out of his body.)

I concentrate deeply: he asks, *What's wrong. Nothing—I am concentrating.* I am finding lines and patterns and things that do not fit the patterns that I find. I outline bones with my thumb, my fingers. I charcoal-sketch the entire skeletal system on skin. And I hear the bones or the spaces between them. Or I feel them separate by the millimeter or twist on each other, like animals not rightly mated.

We sat at the park. We ate sandwiches by the baseball diamond. We wrote in the sand with a short stick, and we wrote in the sand with our fingers.

(We were being childish.)

The time was surrounded, defined, was bookended by work, by hard manual labor and treadmill-like walking, not travel-walking, not destination-pointed. But childish anyway. And that particular novel smile and that always-new, surprising way he watches.

I told him I like the sounds of a fair. (I do, really.) We don't much enjoy fairs anymore, though. But last night, eating sandwiches, we were between a baseball diamond and a festival, and I wanted to take him—to find the entrance and enter, then ride the carousel without horses, that ride where you stand and are kept in only by centripetal force, and ride the Ferris wheel that spun too fast and was not romantic but would keep spinning the two of us up and then down past the ride operator who would inevitably look at us and we would be uncomfortable because we are going so fast and we want it to slow down so we can take in the view and take in each other and finally have a place where we can touch each other the way you want us to touch before you have to go back to work.

I don't think there are any appropriately romantic Ferris wheels in Chicago. Despite the fact that Ferris wheels *are*, supposedly, romantic and despite the fact that the first was created here, in Chicago. Many have since been built, of which I know nothing. There is *the* Ferris wheel at Navy Pier. Of course. The first Ferris wheel no longer exists, taken down and moved and demolished, but this one was not moved, was not demolished, still exists. (For now.) But it is hot and expensive and finances are never romantic and it is crowded and crowds are violent and loud and slow and the line is long and we hate waiting because we are impatient and the apparatus is too slow and too metal and too new and upkept and you are too well caged-in and secure and you feel the security, but I don't want to, I just want to sit, and don't you risk being in that cage with strangers. But the view is nice. The view from there is romantic and endless (at least in one direction).

I do not often look out at that line where the sky drops down behind the curve of the perfectly level surface of a lake. I have, and I can describe it to you; but now all I want to do is steal him away and sit him down and force him to watch me build him a Ferris wheel that goes slow but not too slow and will not go fast and does not have cages and looks old but secure and is painted ivory and lime and strawberry and delirium. And I desire simply the act of building him something. I cannot let him help, but he will try to, and he will ultimately do it himself anyway. (I am somehow weak and submissive.) I want to do it for him, to break (my own) fingers and tear off nails and scratch (my own) skin (in places other than my chest) and burn shoulders (again (with heat, not sun) (yes, with sun)). I do not want to be in pain for him (again), but I want him to know that I would burn myself for him, scratch my skin for him, lose nails for him, that I would sweat for him—so much sweat for him—that I would build a Ferris wheel for him. And ride it with him and look out at that slightly curved line.

He showed me again how to roll cigarettes. I learn a little better each time, I think. He might disagree. But he often sees progress where I do not. This time: start in the middle. You poke it down and roll outward, lightly. Allow the paper to pack the tobacco, not the pressure from your thumbs. You can pack too tightly, press into too perfect a shape. When you do, it is a slow impossible burn, and you have to relight. And when you come to that part where you did not squeeze too tightly or too much (and that is always in the middle), the smoke rushes in, and everything before and everything after feels a waste.

When you are comfortable with the cylinder, stick your fingers in. Press down. Press down hard. When you are comfortable with the cylinder, roll the paper back and stick your fingers in. Then fold.

It is that folding I do not like. After all that rolling—it is always too much rolling for me—I don't like folding, because I think it makes the cylinder misshapen. There is the desire to construct perfectly. I pinch it, and I slide the paper with my index fingers over my thumbnails. Then I pull them out. And then I roll and unroll and roll.

I cannot do this when he is watching me, because I try too hard to impress, perform beyond skill. I try too hard and I press

too hard and it is pregnant or loose or too solid, too uniform to
allow such smoldering to permeate, to blaze at all.

I must have done better this time. He didn't say a word. If I
had fucked up, he would have smiled or furrowed his brow or
said, *Here let me do it* or tell me again how to do it better, the
same way I did it, or tell me to start over.

All I was told was to start in the middle.

It has been intolerably hot in Chicago. For the first time, I was
asked to have lunch with him. It would be brief, and it would be
hot. We sat in a childless playground, the only shade we could
find. We sat on a manhole cover. He told me that I had been
quiet recently. *What's wrong.* I had to make a point of talking.

I told him that I wrote. I told him that I want to build for him
a Ferris wheel. I do not think I said I wrote that I want to build
for him a Ferris wheel. The statements were only consecutive,
although the meaning is the same.

I told him I want to build for him a Ferris wheel, and I told
him how I feel about Ferris wheels and about Ferris wheels in
Chicago. He understood. He said, *If it was ours, we could stop it
while we were at the top, and we could have sex there.*

I said he really *did* understand, only a little surprised at how
easily I could lie.

I saw a car that was not a police car, but I knew it was a police
car by the antennae: no matter the car, no matter the paint on
the car, no matter the people in the car, the antennae are identi-

fiable. It passed, and it stopped. The car backed up, and I knew it was backing up, but I continued to focus on him. I knew that we would be called *gentlemen* and I knew the police officer would identify himself as *police* and I thought this might ruin our lunch, but I didn't say anything, because I didn't want to disrupt (be responsible for the disruption of) the conversation. I needed to see him seeing me see him, seeing me hear him and what he was saying, hearing me respond to him. I did not draw attention to the police car that was not a police car, and all I did was turn my head to the right to see the car back up behind us in my periphery and once I knew it had backed up, I looked forward and I responded to him.

He tells me to follow him. We enter his work. I lose sight of him behind customers and shelves of products. There are so many more customers than normal. They are coming and they are going and they are holding conversations I cannot hear. He disappears behind a customer who is quite close to me. He re-appears on the other side. He is wearing a tuxedo. It is ugly and vertically striped and loose and the pants and the coat are indistinguishable (except the coat is on his top and the pants are on his bottom). The stripes are thin and white but even from a distance, I can see they are not pinstripes. He ducks behind more customers and I catch a glimpse of him climbing stairs. As soon as I realize his work does not have stairs, does not have carpet, does not have mirrors or customers or gold things or handrails or—it's obvious that he is surprising me.

I am not dressed for a wedding. He changed so quickly. He takes extra clothes to work. There is nothing for me to change into. And everyone knows, but everyone is silent. At the top of the stairs, I look for him, but he is gone. There are doorways around which I cannot see and people that create a sort of path that is not a path because they are people and people move and moving things do not make for accurate paths. He is not *gone*, just unfound. On the second floor, there are more people than expected. But he is surprising me with our wedding, and I do not want to complain or do anything that might stop it. I just want to find him. I want to discover what it will be like to have a ring placed on my finger and have it stay there and have it not be temporary and have it be mine. What would it be like to have a ring bought for me, placed on my finger, worn forever. Does a wedding ring feel differently than a normal ring, a father's ring, a ring given with good intentions but at any moment other than engagement or nuptials. There is no fear. Smiling, because I know people around me know, and I want them to know that I know now too. I am smiling, because I want them not to know that I have lost him. I am angry at them all for getting in my way, for walking or standing in any path that might lead me closer to him. But ultimately I do not know which path to take, because I do not know where he went and cannot tell where he has been. (I am looking for him.) I have become desperate, because I just want so badly to marry him. I do not want to walk, I do not want to run, I do not want to hunt or seek or find. I hope that with each corner I turn, I will arrive next to him in his vertically striped tuxedo and he will be on my right and he will turn his head to the left to look at me and he will look at me, and we will be getting married. But this corner is not that corner. But I am telling myself that there are only so many.

He said he could not imagine being with anyone else. (He has been with so many *anyone else*s.)

He said he liked that we do not have to hide anything. Then I shared the things that were as close to *deep* and *dark* as I could. I could not, because I keep things neither *deep* nor *dark* with him. I am always surface. I am always conspicuous. I am always open. And I told him, *I am always open.*

We planned how we will decorate our new apartment. Brick-scheme, brown-and-teal, almost-purple-gray-and-purple. And we talked about our life fifty years from now. So much depends upon hardware and life expectancy.

I told him the story of him. I told him the story of us. *You might know him. We love each other, and we have a dog. We've told each other that we can't imagine ourselves with any other people. We could before, with other people, but not now, now that we're with each other. He and I are getting married. We've already asked each other, and we both said yes. So I guess we might be engaged. He might be my fiancé. Do you know if you can be engaged to someone if there is no ring.*

But aren't the words enough. There is the promise.

I will build him a Ferris wheel right here, here, where we live, butted up against the lake.

We found an apartment against the lake. When we first saw

it—*viewed* it, as it were—we went there, to those rocks, and we sat on them, those rocks that fall straight into the water. The ones that were landscaped, though perhaps carelessly (meant to look careless). (Natural.) But the stone is fake or foreign. Chicago used to have neither beach nor rocks. But the perimeter of Lake Michigan is so convincing that I thought we were sitting on something natural and corrupted and breaking on the very edge.

That day, the waves were small and many and very far apart.

I want to count the miles we can see. I want to count the strokes it would take to get there, how long the sailboat floats and is pulled to get to the point where we see it sitting on a flattish curved line, drawn by a child.

I would carve out seats from those rocks, those boulders. And I would find the fattest, thickest screws and drills and I would attach them to thin and strong strips of metal, and I would round some, and I would bury some, and I would lift each piece by hand (my hands)—the way he and I moved into this place, by hand and alone. And sweating.

I do not know if he is telling himself that he is building anything for me. I think he is building for me (he tells me that he is), but we build so differently that I cannot say with certainty that he is not building for *us*. (He would not build for only himself—that is what he tells me, but I tell him that I won't, but I do (I build for myself)). But we are building simultaneously and concurrently and adjacently and, perhaps, circuitously.

And we ignore the sweat and we wash off the sweat and it keeps developing and the only time we leave it on us, on our backs and hands and crotch and underarms, is when we are too busy to stop building. We want it done. (We are impatient.)

I want that lake to be the washed-off sweat. I have not tasted his—not very much at least, only that which develops quickly while we are differently building—or tearing down and propping up. But I want to drink it. And perhaps this is the reason why I want to offer mine to him. Because I want his, and if I want his, why wouldn't he want mine (he would *not* want mine). And maybe that is why we wash: so that we don't have to drink each other.

If I can't taste the real thing, his real sweat, I want that taste to be simulated by that water and those rocks and the sun and hours of.

It's like you want to submerge me, to hold me still. But you are so willed, so strong in that desire, that you are accidentally drowning me. But I can hold my breath for a long time.

Every night, he falls asleep. I am behind him, or he is resting on me. Every night, he asks, *Baby, can you caress me.* Most nights, he only asks, *Baby.* I do not answer, I just begin. Not because I know, not because he asks. I begin, because I have always wanted to.

I caress most of him. But he asks for back or arm or butt or ear or neck or *play with my hair*. And I want to caress all of him at once or each and every part of him consecutively. (If he did not ask, I would get there.)

He cannot be aware of just how long I do this. After he has fallen asleep. An hour, sometimes. He falls asleep, and I caress him. *Caress* is *his* word. I do not consider my actual movements to be *caressing*; it is not for him, there is no favor. I am being selfish.

I touch him, because I am attempting to memorize him, perhaps expecting to lose him.

Last night it was his hair. The texture, the smell, the length, the amount. Where it grows and where it does not. And today I could smell him on the pillow for the first time.

Every night, I run my palm and my relaxed fingers along his side. His left side. Armpit to hip. This is my favorite—that curve (that curve that changed and disappeared (the one I have not seen in four months but could draw for you still)).

I imagine outlining him. I picture silhouette. And this is the real desire: I want to *know* his body, and I want to be the only one who is able to describe its perimeters, its limits. (Never a possibility.) I want to be the only one able to wrap descriptions around his mitochondria, his throat and his crown and his abdomen and the small of his back, his fingers, his ribs and esophagus, his previously twice-ingrown toenail, all his carbon.

I want to know every atom of him, and I want to control the pleasure of each. And I want that pleasure to be immense, each nerve ending getting the message of me—sensing me and nobody else (sometimes, there were others) and becoming used to me (yes), familiar and comfortable with me.

The way he shies away from my navel-grazing less when he is drunk. The way we ask each other to relax, you know I am not going to hurt you.

I thought it would happen as in a myth.

We arrived, and, just as quickly as we consecrated, we began.

He was on his knees, cleaning all our floors with oil, while I slowly scraped hair and dust from the bathroom's radiator.

The radiator was small, but its pile of dirt was larger than what we collected from the floors, larger than what we collected from all the other radiators combined.

The radiator is small, and it is covered, and it's in a small room. It seems that no matter how often we frequent a space, when there are things to be done, we forget all that lies in the periphery.

We first sat on large light-colored rocks facing the full expanse of the lake, he to my left; the beach, my immediate right. This is our eastern border, our limit. This is how we first came to love.

We list various occasions to return, and we say we will.

It is behind me now, and I have only been there that one time.

Coronis

I pretend a doorway is him, and I dance with it.

A Maenad drinks and dances well and loses her senses. Maenads slaughter voraciously in torrents of blood and meat, making a mess of everything, rubbing viscera over all of this.

When we are dancing, I do not dance the way I do with that doorway. So he tries to get me drunk. I know that everyone should vanish, that it should be just me and just music. I should feel rhythm and beat and lyrics, loudly. I should dance with that doorway. But when I dance with him, I dance with *him*, and there are never any doorways. And when I dance with him, I do not want to dance. Because I never want to dance, only to dance with doorways. And I don't know if this means I am raving or not anywhere near raving enough to show him how much I have dedicated myself to him.

Someone lied—someone who loved him, but did not. He speaks the name, and I am filled with so much rage that I want to nail his extremities to a plank and tear out those nonvital parts—his tongue, his appendix, a kidney, toenails and fingernails, squares of skin, and then replace it all with halite crystals. I am filled with so much rage that I wish he would do the same to me.

He says that he can forget this past servant, but he does not, and I never will.

He used to live on ecstasy and alcohol. Nauseating, to imagine him without control. The irrationality, the overestimation of intellect, the falling and stumbling, the marks on the walls, disorientation, the vomit. And the violence. I think he should have control, but the control he demonstrated was ecstasy. I am nauseated at the thought of a pure tablet of anything, a single-serving anything, because it can be made that simply. Chemical and unemotional, a reaction to many things: lies and disappointment, promises and neglect. And I am jealous. I am jealous for never having experienced that kind of ecstasy. Lies and neglect, promises and disappointment, yes, but never that kind of ecstasy.

I envy. So much and so often. His body is a tool; mine, a weight, something to fight against. He is physical; I am all mythology. He seems to allow himself to have fun, and I write about wanting to have fun. And this is a point of contention.

He is a god of frenzy, a god of epiphany. Random. Luck. In a way, I sought him out. But, in a way, it was entirely possible to have missed him. In a way, he could have chosen not to choose me. We perhaps should have missed each other, for there are so few gods and so many people willing to worship.

I do not know if soulmates exist. If they do, is yours still yours if you do not meet, if, by chance, you think someone else is, if you make someone else your soulmate first. What if the person dies, and you fall in love again. Was it the first or the second, and have either been love. But he did not die, and I will not let him. Love is this: never allowing rigor mortis to set in.

He says he is attractive and will never want for attention. It's true. He has been flocked to, paid for, and could be again while I am forgotten, invisible.

Neptune's wrath. There was a burnt and earthen snake-child in a basket. We are not to look at that which springs from the ground. But her sisters looked. They fled, and she fled, but she did not look, but she watched them look. Sight was her transgression.

Athena gave her wings so she might flee Neptune. She was given wings, depicted as coming out of her back, like an angel, but she was not an angel. She was transformed into a raven. But so slowly. She had wings first, but they could not have come from her back: they must have been her arms (homologous anatomy). Adding is never transmuting, so her wings did not grow from her back, unless she cracked open like a cicada and emerged from herself. And maybe she did. Maybe she became malleable within a shell and squeezed out, wings first. But perhaps her arms changed into wings, and perhaps feathers slowly crept across her shoulder blades and united then traveled down and made a tail. And she was still running (fleeing) because she was still too heavy, and, under the force of an outstretched leg, her knee bent backward, broke, then healed with a bulbous scale.

Then the other. And her black robes melted under sweat and fear and clung to her newly malleable skin. And her bone marrow seeped out of its casing and permanently adhered the robe to her flesh, stitching in and out and deep and surface and all over. She scaled from her feet upward and her new-face emerging from the shell of her old-face became stretched, and as she hardened, her eyes slid to the sides of her head, coated in the blood of metamorphosis.

Newly made light, continuing to buffet her wings, she finally took flight and flew to the woman who saved her.

He is tearing stitches, trying to escape a shell of himself, one to which is so often pointed. (What I mean to say is *I am pointing*, accusing him of his own past.) That shell is dead, dangling from a tree, drowning in New Orleans, and he is still inside of it, but fighting so desperately to get out. And he asks me to see him. I see him struggling, and I am grateful, perhaps, that he has the will and the strength and all that muscle to up and leave if only for the anatomical manifestation.

All that muscle to be violent.

Except when that muscle is used and when that weight is thrown around. Except when he loses control, and all that muscle becomes frightening.

Change requires force, it seems. One *forces* crisis, *implements* it. We burn we break we drown we shift alter abandon purchase.

And flying to Athena is the only thing on my mind, and I am willing to make so many changes, just tell me what, I will do it, so that I may be granted my wings, so that I can break from my shell quickly enough that my wings don't become partially trapped and deformed and useless.

I will break from myself for you. I will break myself. For you.

We are continually changing, he said. *Look at us.* And he goes to the mirror, and I wonder if he is watching himself change in real time. I don't see change that way. I know the beginning, and I see an end, and that end is always never an end but just another still.

The beginning and the end, I have learned, do not have to be distant. The past is anything before now, and things do change slowly.

But now I see the scales developing on my side, below my rib cage. I looked a day apart, in the mirror, and noticed change. Then half a day, change, then less and less until it became that I was watching the reddening scales creep from my spine to my sternum as it happened. I pause, and I interrogate the pain, never as much as childbirth, but a one, then a two, then a three, and here it throbs, here it stabs, there it is a wet itch, there a bruise, a break, a burn. Shingles, my week of crying on and never leaving the couch. A slow, painful metamorphosis.

I imagine what it must be like to look in the mirror on ecstasy.

Nothing would be fast enough to blur the glass, to smear that image, to alter it to impermanence and unreality and wipe it clean, to forget it. It is just before you, and you do not think to look away. You stare, but you want to see your face crack open and emerge from itself. More, and it is already blurred, but because you are blurring too, you do not see the blur: you blur the same blur as everything, so the perception is of a world of solid lines and boundaries.

❧

She is now a raven on Athena's right forearm. His punishment for her is to be black and unable to do anything but tell stories.

All punishments, enabled.

She is lucky as her and six other women's names and seven men's names were chosen *before* all the rest. Coronis was boxed and shipped to Crete and ingeniously placed in a labyrinth. And that labyrinth did not have many ways to go, but only one way to go, forever, forever holding your left hand to the left wall and walking, making the turns you know you don't need to but do for due diligence, so that, just in case there is an exit, you eventually find it. But the Minotaur is lucky too, and he found all fourteen of them, and he would plow through them, driving a horn through the chest of one, stomp heavily on the femur of another, and come eventually to her. She is lucky, and she was not outright killed, but tossed against the left wall, the same to which she managed to keep her hand. And as she was split and gnashed at and horned, she waited for her rescuing, for her transformation. And there was blood pooling to his feet until she had transformed, luckily, to so many disparate pieces and fertilized the ground underneath with sodium and chloride, lipoprotein, fructose and flagellates.

He asks me how one can sit and tell stories for so long. He watches someone do it, and he says he does not know how a person does it. I tell stories. I say, *There is ball-throwing. There is staring out the window.* I say that there is starting over and revisiting and creating new and slaughtering innocents. Type the same sentence over and over, and it becomes deformed.

There is no accurate storytelling except from witnessing the story unfold. Present tense. Everything else is distortion. Everything else is just words. One must be present to understand anything at all.

He cannot leave anything imperfect. He begins again. And his ecstasy must be perfect, and I wonder if I have seen it. If I have seen him give it to others or if I am blind to it when he gives it to me because it is too close upon which to focus. Were I blind in one eye, I may not deal in depth.

❧

Orpheus is a prophet. Orpheus is a poet. And he is Eurydice too. And I would sing to the gates of the Underworld to melt the very hinges, set fire to that wood, and force it open with torrents of tears. I would compose so beautifully that even stones would weep, like this. I would put the dogs to sleep so I may pass so I could see him. All for Eurydice.

He says there are three euthanasias scheduled for today, and I can't stomach it.

Orpheus honored Dionysus until he didn't, until he chose to disdain the worship of any god but Apollo.

Apollo loved Coronis.

He gave Coronis a raven. A star raven, an eleven-starred raven. The raven who was to fetch water, but did not. The raven who was to fetch water but stopped to eat figs. The raven who lied and said it was the snake. The raven who Apollo threw into the sky for having lied about the snake. And he threw there the snake and a cup too. A cup, full, but out of reach. So the raven is up there, dehydrated. A single venom drop to come from the fang of a snake dangling somewhere over. As torture. Until he is freed.

He wants something, and I want something too. And so often, because we both want to be given that which we desire, we go without. And I think sometimes we intentionally starve ourselves so we want it more, so that *want* becomes *need*. But then we both need something we cannot give ourselves, and instead of giving, we wait to receive. And starve.

He told me once, *I could leave you so easily.* And I thought, *What does it mean that I couldn't, as easily.* This uncertainty resulted in broken glasses and doors and glasses and mugs and phones and everything perpetually breaking; several deep reds, pain. But there was a line, and, once there, it *was* easy.

Coronis fell in love with Ischys. And the raven informed Apollo. And Apollo did not believe. The raven was making things up, telling a story, had told it imperfectly. (Tell it again.) So he was cursed. The raven was cursed with so much force that his very wings were turned to ash. And they regrew, and they regrew from the ash, and the ash provided nutrients and dye. And the newly grown feathers were black. The raven was cursed with so much force that every atom mutated. Its gametes, all already there or possibly more to come, became hardened and ghostlike, dark and translucent, jagged and lubricated. The raven was cursed with so much force that even its children and its children's children and all of everything that descended from it was similarly cursed.

Eve had a raven, and it was black.

It must be rare to see an albino raven. But maybe it is not as rare as I think. Its blackness would not increase the rarity of the mutation. Maybe they are as frequent as albino mice. (But those are bred to be albino, for the *purity.*) One in seventeen thousand, and there are so many more than that, but I like to think about mathematics, even though I so often do so incorrectly, even though I am so often wrong, and this *one in seventeen thousand* seems so *possible*.

I type it into a calculator: 1/17000. This should give me a percentage—I should be able to tell you the percent of albino mammals, tell you the percent of albino mammals living, at this very moment. But the answer it gives is 5.8823529411764711e-5.

I don't know what that means. I do not think it is a wrong answer, but I think that I am thinking incorrectly about prevalence and probability. *Am I likely to encounter one.*

I (apparently, like other mammals) had a 1/17000 chance of being albino. The next person to appear—any *next person* would do—I think would be 2/34000. But this is not the case: flip a coin, and the odds are always 50-50 (which is not the same as 50/50). No matter how many times you get tails, the next is only as likely as it has always been to be heads.

We are told it is an albino dog, but he informed me that it was not an albino dog at all. Albinism is *without pigment*, and the hair was white, and neither of us knew if it had pigment, but the *eyes* had pigment. Even the lightest of blue eyes have pigment, and this was proof that there was pigment in the dog. Red eyes are not red, but bloody.

Albinism destroys hiding. It destroys camouflage. Regardless of frequency or prevalence, the lack of pigment means we are easily seen, easy to spot, hunt, kill.

I think of white and black butterflies in a forest, what were they called, and that forest burned to nothing but cinders and ash and soot. The forest was now black, so only the black-and-white butterflies that were mostly black survived, passed gametes, and the species became another, a black or mostly black species.

Ravens are black. And they exist just fine. Despite lack of camouflage.

It is not that Orpheus stopped honoring but that Orpheus disdained the honoring of the rest. There is only one. The singular. One person, is it.

And I am told that there cannot be just one. I am asked to allow for plurality. But I cannot allow for plurality. I am not plural. I have one story and only it to tell and to create. One story, one word. And it seems safe to only be singular, to be as singular, as momentary, as right-now, as *here* as possible. To conflate and overlap and become concentric, but then reduced.

It frightens me when we are more than two, when two bodies possess a third. Attention is divided and split, and it means that one body receives less attention than it would have singularly. 1/1 or 1/2 (or is it *1/1 or 1/3*). To share is to give less care. To care less.

They killed Orpheus for disdaining the honoring of any god other than Apollo.

The Maenads killed Orpheus for vowing to never love another woman.

Eurydice died. She left. To the Underworld. Orpheus failed to get her back. I would have done better. He looked. He looked back, so she remained dead. I would have torn out my eyes so that I would not look back, so that I may be with you, be with you even without seeing you. I want to see you, but I would do anything to be with you. I would sing and dismember myself. For you. So he vowed to never love another woman, to never have sex with another woman. So if you died, I would vow to never love another woman, I would vow to never have sex with a woman. He did not vow to never love another man, to never have sex with another man. And love is not in this part of the story, but sex is, and he had it, but not with Eurydice, and not with any other woman.

Orpheus, the first sodomite.

So the Maenads killed him. They eviscerated him. The Maenads shredded his flesh around his joints, and they pulled knob from socket and knob from socket and knob from socket and they suckled on those garnet protrusions. They spread him open by their nails and they used their nails to cut him open, anything but clean, but pouring mildew and saliva and blood and salt down the open wound, and they removed each organ, and they wrapped their tongues around his teeth and testes and pulled and pulled until the tissues finally gave, and there were roots and strings attached, and they fell to the ground, where they accrued grass and dirt. The Maenads sawed off his head. They left it intact, aside from the teeth. Unmarred. Beautiful. Mouth agape and wagging tongue.

Carrion

A cat could not have done it, not in such a manner: she'd have had plumes stuck between her pointy, yellowed, newly rounded teeth and bird matter matted to her yellow fur and paws. Her claws would have penetrated the bird too deeply and too frequently, from trying desperately to hold onto this thing she loved. Instead of holding, drowning—suffocating. Her curved sewing needle nails would have eviscerated, making a mess of all this. This, however, was too clean of an operation.

On the train, there was a pale man with a mustache. It wasn't until much later that I recognized his pallor. I watched him put away the newspaper he had been reading, close his eyes, and stretch his knitted cap over his head. He stood up between stations, which seemed odd to me at the time, not yet accustomed to Chicago public transit. He folded himself into a ninety-degree angle, torso parallel to floor, and vomited at the door of the train. He was ashamed, I presume, hanging his head low so as not to allow others to see. But the index was there, slowly crawling along into the aisle.

Birds are oil and rubber and grease and shrapnel. They rock themselves along sidewalks and perch themselves perfectly atop anything, over anything dead. But their movement is mechanical, too organized. Birds do not seem to lose balance, they do not seem to become sick, they do not fall; they know heat patterns and weather patterns and all kinds of patterns, and they follow these unnamed, undetermined things as if programmed to do so. They are computer chips and matrix, not blood. Not really. So there would have been none for a cat to spill, and this fact was reflected, perhaps, by the pristine sidewalk. Birds are not humans, and I know this, because when a cat drags her nails across our chests, slowly enough to deceive us of depth, blood pools at our sternums, if only afterward.

Two men in soiled T-shirts and trucker caps destroyed cement steps with a jackhammer. Right near them was an old man, dressed to stay out in this fall weather for more than a few hours. Cardigan, earmuffs, possibly a hat, comfortable shoes. Many layers. He swept dust from the cracked, uneven sidewalk between his house and theirs. And I imagine that he would be at it all day, Möbiusly sweeping as more dust accrued.

The wings were somehow seemingly preserved. They were intact and pulled taught, choreographed to mimic life, flight—stick-straight and childlike. But they were beautiful, opalescent and changing color enough to signify movement, as if they could have been attached to something still, albeit something made immobile. Concrete-filled. Iron and wood and carbon. Trojan. They were unsurprising, those wings, lying on the sidewalk. They were exactly what I would have thought of—indeed, what I likely *have* thought of—when I imagine bodiless wings. Except for those two bulbous protrusions, those cartilageless balls. Wings are clipped, and they are flat. When I think of the anatomy of a bird, I do not think of joints or sockets: the bird is always either whole or already completely ravaged.

The man stopped moving the broom only long enough to look up and smile at me. The noise his broom no longer made in the early dawn told me the whole story: he had no idea of what was on my mind:

Could I do it. How much force must be used to tear off the wings of a bird, and is that force different if you pluck one from one side and then the other from the other; or, if you use opposing forces, is that number smaller. Is dismantling an animal, making it its component parts, a matter of strength or of guts. Is it firm grasp and pinching, muscle, bone, and immediate shredding. Facing me or away. Alive or already dead. Or is it more similar to watching a snuff film or those beheading videos released a few years back. You sit at your computer, press play, then just don't stop it. You can. But you don't. You wait it out—a painfully slow process from initial slash, blood beginning to pump out through the hole in the vein and then out through the newly made end of the vein, pumping out beat after beat and falling down his torso, to sawing of vertebrae—eventually, but it just takes so long—until only the head is held by its hair, blue eyes staring at you, slack-jawed and wagging tongue. Just to see it through. Just to say you have.

Those five or six slabs of cement were, I saw the next day, turned to ash. To say *rubble* does nothing to convey that it was dust, that it was four pounds of carbon and calcium. And of course, I thought of the sweeping old man. And where was he now, now that the work was done, the cleaning now necessary and able to be completed without having to start over. And where did he sweep it to. And how long would it take to clean up these remains.

And just how long does it take to—to what. To build new steps or to clean. Or to adjust to there no longer being steps at all. I don't know which, and, regardless, I do not yet know the answer.

But I imagine that ripping off the arms of an animal would be like pulling out a tooth. Your own, a loose one, only a little gum partially adhered; only sinew and skin keeping it in that socket, covered in feathers. Perhaps frightening, especially that first time, if you do it yourself and it doesn't just fall out, but at some point, you gather the strength to just do it. Then the rubies are exposed, moist and round and polluted with the fiber and tissue that did not separate. And you salivate and tongue the wound.

Mother

I used to resent my mother's advice—all those responses to prove that things are manageable when that is not how they seem. I used to think it was a product of being rural, a sign that we were a family who wasn't smart enough to seriously, intellectually, rationally consider real-life matters; that the only thing we had at our disposal was country wisdom, not book smarts, not science, not being cultured. I resented how it felt like a belittling or a sweeping simplification. But now that I am two states away from her and speaking to her at length only once a week and seeing her maybe three or four times a year, I have grown to appreciate the colloquial, the folk wisdom.

I assume she has thought herself able to summarize a dilemma or trauma or question into a prepackaged sentiment, a formulated phrase, because these are the same she heard from her own mother for similar circumstances. As a family, growing up and, it seems, through generations, this is what we had: hand-me-downs.

Wes, I wish you wouldn't put all your eggs in one basket.

The trouble I have with her advice is that it is actually neither insensitive nor an oversimplification. My trouble is that I'm coming to terms with the reality of my situation, as others see it. That is to say, she is right: I *do* put all my eggs in one basket. She says this, and I cry the next day, only now able to see that she has indexed something that has always been true about me:

I have *always* placed all of my eggs in one basket. My trouble, then, is not knowing how not to do this.

Before now, I've not considered what it means. Instead, I have just always already known, instinctually. But I don't *really* know: placing all of one's eggs in one basket could be bad, because if something happens to that single basket, all of those eggs are lost or, what might be worse, broken. These eggs are our food, our finances, our well-being and valuables, and they are our relationships. We are walking along a dirt road or through the woods alongside a dirt road, and we trip. And the eggs fall. And they are all lost to us. So we must learn—the lesson of this proverb is—to separate our eggs: place one in my left pants pocket, one in my left hand, one nested on my tongue, and the basket, now with fewer eggs, may be carried between right hip and right hand. If I trip, I would hold up the egg in my hand to save it. Both arms thus occupied, my face would slap against the small broken twigs and leaves and dirt previously underfoot, and my torso would crush the basketed eggs. Perhaps the egg in my mouth could resist the force of impact—my own fat wagging tongue.

But saying *one* basket as opposed to *the* basket sounds like we are to separate our eggs into multiple wicker baskets: keep a basket on your head, another between right hand and hip, another between left hand and hip, one more slung over shoulder. But if I trip, they are all still lost to me. I do not have enough hands to monitor the uprightness of more than one basket.

The proverb does not hold. It *cannot* hold. Because *I* cannot. I don't know that I can find a logical explanation for having more eggs in more baskets. And, frankly, I do not understand how anyone *could*. It is unwise, as one would be spread too thin: each egg would receive less attention. The likelihood of breaking becomes greater, the chances of hatching, smaller. With more objects, we are more divided.

What I know is that I have always only wanted one basket—or, more likely, only one egg. A mythically large egg. The appropriate proverb or command would be to only have one egg in which you can invest all your energies, that you can protect, to which you can give all your attention. It is, I think, the same biological logic for carrying so few fetuses at once: we are not kangaroos and do not have the ability to eject (abort) that which we know will not survive the drought. We can only carry so many things to term.

But this is that thinking: only having one egg is equivalent to placing all of my eggs in one basket. As if many robin eggs have been pressed together, transformed into a single roc egg. I am sure there is a mathematical explanation for this equivalency, but I don't know what that might be—but I *know* that only having one egg *is* the same as having all one's eggs in one, centralized place. So even as I recognize that she is right, I approach the very words my mother provides with the logic she is warning against. Yes, if I have more eggs, there *is* the possibility for more to survive, but there is also, mathematically, the possibility for more to be lost. But this is all only *possible*.

Despite the distortion of echo or memory, vibrating and shortening, I know one thing clearly: how I typed it, *Wes, I wish you wouldn't put all your eggs in one basket*, is not accurate. That comma makes it seem like an address immediately preceding the proverb. But it was not. It was *not* a comma, it was an ellipsis, silence. Her saying my name had little to do with what came after.

When she said my name, she was acknowledging that I was upset, saying my name so I could hear it. Because, while those closest to us use our names the least, hearing it is not only comforting because it reminds us that we are someone, suddenly already being and no longer becoming.

Or she was disappointed. The vowel of my name was not upturned, as it would be for an address, but rather fell into that sibilant which lingered perhaps longer than it normally would have. And the silence—there was no silence there: I just couldn't hear that she was sighing. Had I been there, looking at her, recumbent on that dark green couch, facing the television, I know I would have seen her chest lift itself then fall again and her small lips purse immediately after, just before opening again to speak. *Wes.*

I wish you wouldn't put all your eggs in one basket, then, might have been an afterthought.

I have said to those around me, *Tell me what it is like to have more than one friend. What is it like to have more than one person text you. What is like to pay for a phone you use to call more than only three people.* I am curious, because it is an experience I have never had. I thought I was unlikable, not social. But this is not the case.

In my adolescence, there was only one nonfamilial person I ever spent time with. And I was so wholly invested in her as my friend. Until she wasn't anymore. I began to live without a friend—that is, I began to live with no friends other than the goats and ducks and chickens in the backyard, the dog on the couch, and my own family. I didn't search, because I didn't know or remember how to. But as soon as a friendly hand was offered, I clung, fearing there may be no other, fearing if I offered mine in the future, it would be refused. And my hand, under the force of this new friend, was meant to touch, reach out to, hold others'. It was in that way that I realized I needed both hands to hold one, preferably two—that I could not hold, touch, embrace as many hands as others.

And this is exactly what my mother said troubled her: I can hold that one hand only, only if that one hand is holding only mine. But devotion, it seems, is so infrequently equal.

I made only three friends in high school: the only openly gay boy to pass through that damned school system in ten years (my sister graduated with Francis, ten years before; my brother, five years between us, didn't know any gay people—and, when that school is only filled with six hundred bodies, you *would* know) became friends with the obese girl, the goth girl, and the too-bubbly girl with a skin condition. We were friends because we were already outcast and bitter and socially deviant. And that is how my friendships have been: I don't *seek* friends; I befriend those with whom I am forced into proximity. This is how friendship happens in youth: a parent wants to see another parent down the road, so they let their two kids play together, and those two kids only play together because they have to, because their parents want to play together. Friendship, the byproduct of circumstance. Our friendships are all by proxy, in one way or another.

I don't understand, then, the idea of *best friend*, as I've only ever had one true friend with perhaps one or two secondary friends, though the divide between primary and secondary, *best* and not-*best*, is always vast. It is simply easier for me to have fewer close relationships: fewer obligations, more intimacy, better understanding. I don't know how to divide myself.

More than one pattern exists here: all this, and that all of my friends, the close ones, the egg ones, are women—which certainly has something to do with my mother.

She was intolerably close to her mother, which had a lot to do with control. But this closeness was still passed on to her children, only with the power and control corrected for, replaced with support and encouragement. This *closeness* has created a bond with my mother that I can only describe as a friendship. So it's easy to say that all of my closest friends have been women because my first and closest, most intimate relationship—created, of course, by proximity (what would be the chance of my meeting or seeking out my mother were I not her son)—was with a woman.

But I resist using that easy explanation, because while it may be *true*, it is not *entire*. There is more to all of this than that: because I don't know how else to say it—and I fear losing meaning with rhetorical gymnastics—my mother was the only parent I knew.

Or, my mother was the *only* parent I knew.

Or, my mother was the only parent I *knew*.

But the tense of the statement: it's true, my mother *was* the only parent I knew, but she is *still* the only parent I *know*: she did not remarry, and I have kept my father so distant that I don't know that I have yet come to know him.

He left when I was four, I think. He never lived far away from the family, and I saw him every other weekend until I was in my teens. I remember how my mother and father would argue—always about whether or not money was enough to be a parent and how much money and how much caretaking makes you a good parent. Always about kinds of distances. My father seemed largely absent from my life: he always had the proclivity for emotionally vacating before *physically* vacating as soon as I was eighteen and his legal financial obligations were over. Of course, I had a lot to do with another kind of distance: I shut him out, because he hurt my mother. He cheated on her. At least twice. Long affairs. And I still don't know if I have or know how to forgive him.

She taught me how to be a friend, and she taught me to stretch myself thinner than possible for anyone—*bend over backward*, as she would say. Even though she had two other children, she treated me as if I was the only other person in the world. And I didn't know how to do anything other than reciprocate. I was her one egg, or I was treated as such (that seems to be the power of the love of a mother), and she was mine for a very long time.

I rarely hear of positive relationships with fathers—they abandon, abuse, neglect, are hated—but they are nonetheless important. At least as important, in our typical heteronormative sense, because parents are always models for how to live one's life, if only because they are our first interpersonal interactions. While the relationship with my mother gave me the ideal, a form after which to sculpt all others, the best-case scenario for maintaining relationships, for egg-tending, the *right way*, my father gave me—something else. He taught me what to fear, what happens when relationships turn to ruin under the weight of one's own infidelity and selfishness, when arrogance tells me everyone will return to me, flock to me. He taught me what happens when we believe we have everything under control— but we don't. He also taught me that I can tell someone to leave.

Whether it was because he already had two children or because he already had a son, he did not want a third child. But my mother did. I never understood what happened between them, but I am here, and that can only mean that my mother lied about being on birth control or otherwise duped my father into thinking they would or could have no more children. I know that they talked about it—I trust my mother when she says that they did and that he was adamant about not having another child. But how she conceived me is so hard to imagine, because my mother has never seemed to me the kind of person to lie about matters of such consequence—which is, again, why I believe her when she tells me that my father did not want to have me. The only *gain* she could have gotten from telling me such a lie would be my favor, but she had that long before I was ever told.

My brother was the favorite. Middle child. Once I discovered that my sister was not my father's (because my brother and I did not grow up with this knowledge) and that I was unwanted, I mentally revisited certain events and found *this*, not favoritism. I continued to remember or uncover things. For example, the first time I watched a home movie after coming to this knowledge:

My brother, Tobi, and I play in the back yard where we kept our goats. Cloudy day, green grass, beat-up, homemade fence. My father speaks from behind the camera to my brother and encourages him to do one thing or another—to perform. My brother does not appear enthusiastic, perhaps even stifled by my father's expectations. My voice is heard from off-screen. A little voice with a speech impediment, asking my father to record *me*. This could easily be the product of my being five years younger than my brother, an age when I may have *wanted* to perform where and when he did not. The camera stays on my brother, unwavering. My brother sways defeatedly, now looking at the grass, now a goat, but not the camera. My voice is heard from off-screen again and then a third time. My father, reluctantly: *Okay, Wesley, but hurry up.* Camera pans right, to me, at the base of a slide. With my slippery little kid shoes, I stumble slowly up the swing set's ladder, the same that the goats scratched with their horns, either for marking their territory or because they itched—I have never determined which. I climb not even halfway up the metal slide before the camera pans left, back to my brother. My little voice asks, *Did you see me.* Even if he did, the camera he held did not.

The relationships with my parents have instilled two fears in me: a fear that someone will always rob me of desire—steal desire away from me, distract from me, make me feel inferior, as if I am not good enough for him—and a fear that I will be left without explanation.

I have had no choice but to proceed through relationships with these fears, and I have tried to combat them the only way I know how: my mother failed, so I must be better than, more than. I attempt to be more empathetic, more interesting, more generous, more devoted, more attractive, smarter, and more successful. But this has as little to do with my mother as it does the other person—the one who robs me of my relationship, my commitment: he is the one I want to be better than, so that I will not be abandoned at all—as if I can prepare for that.

The other, unattractive side of these fears is that I constantly suspect their reality: *Do you like me. Do you love me. Am I ugly. Is he more attractive than me. Why don't you want to have sex with me. Do I have too-big thighs. Did you like it. If you're not doing anything tonight, maybe you'd like to hang out.* And I look—desperately—for signs of extra-relationship desires: *Is he looking at porn. Who does he talk to when he's at work. Is he flirting again. Who has he recently friended. Why is his ex-boyfriend visiting. Why is his ex-boyfriend staying with us. Sleeping with us. Fucking us.* I have been called insecure. And I am.

Of course this is exacerbated by having been cheated on, having been asked to be interested in threesomes as well as in polyamory. Because men *have* grown bored of sex with me. And they *do* leave, if I don't leave them. And now I try to navigate the remains—the cracked shell that my mother and father were able to piece together as a friendship. And, now, I try to forgive my father and formulate that relationship thinking that perhaps I just need one, just one relationship with a man to work unconditionally.

Any relationship I have is boiled down to this egg-basket proverb: I devote myself with so much passion and intensity so quickly—almost immediately—because I seek the one who will not abandon me. I only need one relationship to not break. So I eject—or reject—the deformed ones, the discolored ones, the cracked ones, the otherwise inferior ones from my basket so that I can focus on the survival of one. It is that relationship kept locked between my cracking, crowded teeth. Forcing itself back toward my throat to make room, weighing down my tongue, which compresses itself so that it does not squeeze the egg too tightly against the roof of my mouth. So I travel silently across this dirt road, and I am running. I am running to get as far as I can—hopefully to that end point, that place to where we carry our relationships, that thing or place that I want most from this one relationship—as quickly as I can, hoping to make it there before I swallow, before I bite, before the ground falls out from under me, before I gag, before I am mauled by a cougar, before a tree falls on me, before I am poisoned or bear-trapped. Or before someone comes along and simply tears my mandible from my skull in one deft movement to retrieve that single egg, leaving me standing there bemused, tongue wagging long and wide at my neck.

Mother

after Virginia Woolf

I can't write a single phrase that describes you and me. Approaching the page, I doubt, and I tremble, afraid to make even one sentence. I keep you here on my desk, for reference, for inspiration: a book so underlined (entire pages, double, thrice) that the gesture has become meaningless. But when you inspire, you intimidate. So instead of writing, I look for pictures of you online—perhaps for the one in which you and Thomas walk through the garden, blurry, my favorite.

Instead, I can't look away from this: a photograph that dates you as forty-nine years and eight months old, as in the rest of the album—unaging, static. Except, in this one, you are somehow withered. No visible wrinkles or sunspots, but anything other than the precocious *Jinny* pictured elsewhere. The surprise of your eyebrows doesn't hide that your death is inevitable, historical; but it is awful to see how your body decays. If I could believe that I should grow old in pursuit and change, I should be rid of my fear: nothing persists. *She is dying here*, I want to say, but instead, *She is almost fifty years old* and, in under ten, the door will open and the tiger will leap. Nothing persists.

I know to whom you refer when you say, *You did not see me come.* But I transfer, and I project. You are *you*, and I am *me*, but what is the difference between us. We each lose our hardness, become soft like wax near the flame of the candle. We melt into each other with phrases. We are edged with mist. You are you, though sometimes Stephens; sometimes hard or soft; sometimes dead. You are Rhoda, sometimes, because you composed her, and you composed *as* her. They were all different, but Rhoda, the most alone of them all, the most melancholic; you, their unifying force, all made one—loved undistinguished and common.

I have all but turned you to three kinds of paper and binary now, because I had been trying to meet you singly, again, again. But this time is different. This time, you did not see me come. I circled round the chairs to avoid the horror of the spring. I emptied my attempts of ceremony and embraced the desire to be the same as you, with you, in love with you. (One should never love calmly.) It is anxiety that springs out when I try to meet you only once, wholly. This fear of recognition and dropped veils, a fear of being ghost-like, transparent and predictable. Because the adequate attempt is still so often a failure.

Were you to see me, there would be something uncanny. My nose, my hair, the way we hold our mouths. This is the horror of the looking glass we avoid. Rush past, and take comfort in that you are you and Tom, Percy, Vita. That you are Lytton, Mary, Jane. And maybe I am *I* as much as I am any of you.

It is terrible to see your lives all at once, in one moment. I am afraid of the shock of sensation that leaps upon me, because I cannot deal with it as you do—I cannot make one moment merge in the next, for every moment is singular. To me they are all violent, all separate. A series of now and now and—. If I fall under the shock of the leap of the moment you will be on me, tearing me to pieces. Of this I am sure. Such certainty: if I meet you, you will tear me to pieces. But, if I meet you, I will reciprocate the best I can.

I want to compose a single phrase here describing how you look. My words feel inadequate, so I turn to yours, and I find this: from your diary, dated 29 December 1940, *I detest the hardness of old age—I feel it. I rasp. I'm tart.*

This is four months before you stop persisting, nine years after the photo, though it looks as if you've been rasping all that time. But now, so close: standing at the precipice, rasping. And I cannot help but think of your death, as if it matters, as if a body has anything to do with art, as if your body were your art. Preposterous. I am tempted to find your diary entry. To see if, when we don't finish things, they remain unfinished—to see how we just end. I could traverse four months: it's not many pages, that amount of life. But from somewhere, your voice springs up, and I hear your letter to Leonard. I will end with this instead, for who we are when we are whomever we want to be is so much more threatening than the version we give to others.

But in the photo, it is difficult to recognize you. I myself have not yet withered, so I can't. Not yet. But I have to and want to continue. So.

I would capture her myself. A butterfly collector. I would place her in her library, one that is not also a bedroom, as in Monk's house. I would place her on a stool in her library, and I would tell her to reach with her back arm—it would be her left arm—for Montaigne. But I would not move Montaigne to a higher shelf to achieve this pose. I would capture her reaching for Montaigne, whether she should squat, stand on tiptoe or on stool. I would have her eyes closed, because she knows exactly where it is—she must. He is not forgotten easily: he is well-worn and thumbed and licked-fingered. He is translated.

I would move her desk into her library, were it not already there. On the desk, the manuscript of *The Waste Land*. A photo: Leonard. Tom. Vita. The floor would be old, as old as she, and it would be rubbed and loose like she. I would push the chair in and I would pull it out three thousand times to create the stress on the varnish of the wood floor. I would take a picture of the floor where the chair originally was, before I moved it, and I would paint the floor of the library to look identical, should those three thousand pushes and pulls not suffice.

I would make her wear a cardigan. And I would make her barefoot. And as she posed, I would notice her hair sticking up, flyaways from the wind from the open window, and I would hang the camera from my neck for this moment, for walking over and saying, *Jinny, your hair. It's always your hair.* I would take it down, and I would smooth it back, and I would put it back up and I would smile at her, feeling as though I were taking care of her. I would put it up and realize that I did it all wrong, and I would apologize and I would be so shy, and I would hate to ask her if she would redo it herself, but I would, and she would, and I would begin again, taking pictures with her hair up and disheveled.

And I would leave the shutter open, instructing her to breathe deeply, heavily, so I may capture the semitransparent swell of her chest. *You can blink, please blink—I want you comfortable. I know, it seems strange, because it will be blurry, you will be blurry, but do not pose, not for this.*

She would flippantly say, in her dark, commanding voice, *If you wish to capture me naturally, then let me live naturally. You may leave the shutter open.*

To let her, I would need to mount the camera and leave it there in the corner of the room, staring blankly and widely at some vanishing point it cannot truly see. And I would.

The document would first be mists, blurs, stretches of her across the room. An occasional ghost-like face, then many, then all mists over everything. Then the sun would set, and I would capture a dark room overtop a lit one. The result: a womb-life gray. And this seems fitting, in a way, that specific gray, tinged with not yet being able to print perfect black, bordered in that almost-white. And I would hold it, I would show it to her, and she would say what she would say, and I would reply, *I want to do it again. This time, longer.*

Until when.

I have no end in view.

In this withered, this withering photo, she looks out an open window, ignores the photographer, out over the plowmen. She watches shaking trees and rooks beating up against the wind. *They rise and sink, up and down, as if the exercise rubbed and braced them like swimmers in rough water. But what little I can get down into my pen of what is so vivid to my eyes, and not only to my eyes, also to some nervous fibre, or fanlike membrane in my species.*

As I encounter her now, everything seems to have lost its vividness. She dead-stares. Of course I want her to be looking at the rooks as she says she often does (as she obviously often does), but I just want to see her fixing her gaze on something. She does not look alive enough, enlivened or excited enough to be watching a moth in the window or knots of a huge net falling and then being thrown up with a loud creak and then falling again onto a presumably bare tree. I want to say this is a look of ambivalence, but that is not the word, as that is *both*, not *nothing*. But I don't want *nothing* either—I don't want *apathy*. What is the word for not having the ability to care, not being in control of your faculties enough to even say *I don't care*—because that is the word I want to use to describe how she looks. Vacant. Absent. She is not there.

I wonder if she is thinking in this very moment about ending her life. I do not know how to run minute to minute and hour to hour, solving them by some natural force until they make the whole and indivisible mass that you call life. We solve hours. We solve minutes. There is a problem, an equation, of time and energy and cost and desire, and we solve it. That minute, that second, that single shutter-opening: what is the problem. What solution had she found outside that window.

Yes, Virginia, you are looking at something, and you have solved something. You are pondering something. I can tell you have asked yourself this same question hundreds of times already today, and I want to know what it is. I don't think it is about solving a minute, because you have an end in view.

I would hardly consider anything in her old age to be *hard*: her skin is loose and soft, lightly haired, her bones hide beneath just enough flesh, her fingers are not thin, the chair is stuffed and the fabric is worn. Her old age is softness, not a hardness.

Jinny, your old age is disintegration, not rigidity. You are not yet dead. Not yet. I am going to take care of you for the next and last nine years of your life. And then you will lean against the wind, and then you will become heavy, and you will puff more, and you will be cold, and you will be soft and wet.

One person, is it, to sit beside (yes, Virginia, there is a person), *an idea, is it* (and there is an idea to which I am running), *your beauty, is it* (no, Virginia, I have not been made to believe in that yet). How dare you suggest beauty may be my goal. Though I would like for you to, you do not know anything of me.

This sentence is your most hateful and accusatory, and I have had enough of that. Disdain for, resentment at being part of something so large when you feel so small and light. There are so many times that I am pushed and it hurts in my stomach and shoulders, and it backhands my jaw, and my glasses flip off forever distorted; you could accuse me of anything, you could suggest any three things, and you would be convinced that it would be one of them. I have no say in these matters, because you search through fictions to find the truth. The truth I give to you, and you tell me I am lying, that there is no person, no idea, and I believe in beauty. How can I disprove you when you say that you do not want to be disproven, that this is not about evidence. I do not know. How do I prove to you that I ought to prove to you, that this *is* about evidence, about exhibits, and love and trust.

You berate me for my days and hours passing like the boughs of forest trees and the smooth green of forest rides to a hound running on the scent, as if you did not have a quarry, as if you want my life to be chased through bramble and briar, burs. And perhaps you are right in thinking it should not be all one blurred forest, ought not to be smooth or fast. I don't know forests, not really, only woods, and only cornfields that I have run through. The leaves seem serrated and tinctured: a thin slice with lips that hurts for days, ducking, only offering your face for the densest of the leaves. I should not have been there, but it is no matter, as the cut will never show.

Virginia, I would love to have a forest. Dodging tree trunks and bending under boughs and leaping over animals and downed branches and brooks is preferable to that sting, that slow-moving, laborious caution. Worry and fear make traveling slow. One must move fast to stay on the scent. Send the dogs ahead. I am unable to keep up. I am trying to avoid my neck and wrists from being slowly sliced open, unaware. It is exhausting to run, I know. The pump of leg and heel is all too much for one body, but.

(Sometimes, you just need to run.)

No, you say, *there is no single scent, no single body for me to follow.*

I envy you for that. The glory of being multiple, complex; I know only simplicity, single-union, the limits of a fixed identity; romance, writing romance, teaching romance, the lack thereof. The forest streak you see is not *ease* but multiplicity, mist. You neglect that. I want that joy of being somebodies, plural. I want to be me and me and you and Byron and Percy and Rhoda and

I and *I*. It is troubling to be so few at once. I am so limited, I am nobody; I have no face.

The photo is ethereal: that length of face, the nose, the hair, her posture. She looks haggard, and I can think only of the Angel in the House (you didn't create her): she is tied with Leonard's belt to her wooden chair, the chair bolted up to the desk, and the Angel beating her with a crop, pulling her by her hair to remove her from her seat, gnashing her teeth at her ear and the belt and the paper and the books and the pen, and she screams, *You are ignoring them. They know what you are doing, and it is self-indulgent, verging on hedonism. It is selfish. And you know they feel this way, and you feign being unapologetic. But you wish to apologize. Apologize to them. Stop writing.* She is tied down, and while there is no mechanism to force her to write, she is at the desk, so she writes anyway, as if that violent voice did not matter. She stole it, gave it form, and carried on despite it. So that she might have something for which to fight. She created a force to struggle against.

The Angel is stronger than I am; writing, a chore. I imagine her this way, beaten and melancholic and struggling in her profession, because that is so often how I feel, and I tolerate it only when I imagine this to be the case with her as well. I cannot shrug this Angel, but I know at least that I find comfort in writing, and I need someone to teach me how. *Teach me how to tolerate the screams and the slamming doors, the throwing and the tears. Teach me how to distinguish between what should and should not be ignored; Virginia, teach me how to be as strong as you.*

Here, her hair is the same as it always was, dry and frizzy and somehow kempt. She somehow pulls it back, and individual strands dry up and away from the bun—haloed by her own genetics.

Her mouth. Agape, full lips falling from inevitably stained teeth, gapped, as they look in this photograph, though I do not remember her having a gap—though I do not remember ever having seen a photograph of her smiling, one in which I could see her teeth. (I look, and I see her smiling with Tom, with Lytton.) I imagine her young characters, a young Bloomsbury group, overtly loving each other but with six private lives, separate, distinguished, and anguishing in their losses and disappointments. And how they would smile in public and look like *this* in private.

Her mouth. And a depression in her temple that seems unnaturally, painfully deep, almost as if scarred, a piece of flesh removed then healed over. It looks like damage, a throbbing place. This must have been the source of all those headaches, and I feel I am viewing her from a privileged vantage, able to see exactly where that vulture sits on a bough, where the rat gnaws at her head. I wonder if I was right in first thinking of her death, as this might have been a painful moment, one in which the inevitable catastrophe felt close—her body about to smash itself to smithereens. *Privileged*, because all but her ink-smudged fingers was private. But there is something about living in an odd amphibian life of suffering that makes one take that pain in one hand, pure sound in the other, and clap them together to give language to all this.

Illness, the great confessional.

I am like the foam that races over the beach, able to smooth out those wrinkles, turn Virginia into Jinny again. I want to cover her from sight, keep her private and singular and mine. Or, I am like the moonlight that falls arrowlike here on a tin can, pointing and perhaps taunting. In turning her into binary, into a single image, into many singular images, I am placing her under glass, pinned and slowly dying the death to which she was already succumbing.

All that's in focus is the chair. She is before it, as if the photograph was not meant to be of her at all—before the point from which the lens aligns light onto a single plane. As if she is always too soon. She would have liked this. It would remind her of the eternal procession, of her sister's paintings, of everyone without faces. She was too full of movement to be captured on film rightly. And this is the only aspect that makes the photograph tolerable. She would not only like being but also want to be out of focus, as she should never be the one who is considered, examined, thought about. Only her works.

And yet, here I am.

Here on a spike of the mailed sea holly.

I looked. She wrote, *A curious sea side feeling in the air today. It reminds me of lodgings on a parade at Easter. Everyone leaning against the wind, nipped & silenced. All pulp removed. This windy corner.* I tell myself I understand this—an unnerving idea, less the fact that I live in Chicago, and I live so near the lake.

I saw it for the first time when the clouds were sparse and thinned to nothing, making the lake indistinguishable from the sky, which turned from that sky blue to pale to aluminum. Leaves hovered, gold and bronze and sinusoidal, working the impression of stagnation. The way things there always moved, were always moving. That wrought-iron-finished mild steel has chipped and rusted. Because broken. Because abandoned. I counted (neurotic enough to need to know exactly): waves were ruining themselves against sand and rocks every four seconds, from there to the jagged wooden pier to the north, from there to the even more jagged wooden cordon to the south. I still hear the waves, sometimes, from inside, and I think it is the wind blowing through branches and leaves. But the wind is never blowing in these moments, so it is always just the water molecules constantly pummeling and abrading and bumping and melting together.

I watch water change color. Here, nearest to me, the water is transparent and malleable like glass. But here, nearest to me, air is pocketed and engulfed and drawn and outlined to the point of visibility. I watch water change color. The most notable: a mass exodus of electrons, a shower of copper carbonate, oxidized. And I could rub lemons all over this—*all* this—but I like that color, that form of destruction.

My being here, so close to this water, has brought me closer to you: more water to me than carbon, or a bone or a half-eaten boat.

Her right hand, especially—it is especially blurred. Her hand sooner than the rest of her sooner than the chair. The ring on it. Its position. The tapering of her fingers, how surprising it is to see not a skeletal figure but a fleshy one. And the entirety of the photograph feels so corporeally distorted: her neck is bent a wrong way, and the watch is twisting and pinching the skin of her left wrist; her legs are too long, too big, and her body has always felt so small and light, like mine. I am blown down caverns, and flap like paper against endless corridors.

I must press my hand against the wall to draw myself back. Abrasive and violent and critical. I imagine her telling me my work ought to be sold for only £4.10. Tom's work shook her. (She *was* shakable.) I wonder if this is shaking her. Or did my first time shake her more, or perhaps the year of silence between attempts—and how many more will I make at dislodging her.

But since I wish above all things to have lodgment, I pretend, as I go upstairs, to have an end in view. I believe I learned this from you, that we must trust our selves. That we can let our unfinished work become finished. I hear it, your voice, womb-life-grayed and liquid and certain, with the scent of delphiniums, sweet peas, bunches of lilac, and carnations and moss and London.

I wait for you to speak and then speak like you.

Conflagration

My former belief in metempsychosis had less to do with afterlife than how to live as if we are each always already somebody else—or always never who we once were. So, when I see a black smudge on my desk, some sort of soot smashed into the grain by some book, I intuitively know that it should stay, right where it is; that I should forgo my ordinary neurotic cleaning.

So it remains, surrounded by burnt-black tips of wick and light caramel-colored pencil shavings with deep green scalloped edges. It should all stay, should also remain alongside the burgundy eyeliner pencil sharpener.

I have decided that it *must* stay, because, I tell myself, without having or needing any proof, that this was how writers in the 1920s lived: desks against walls in their small apartments, pencil shavings strewn all across, books with broken spines circumventing all the lined paper. Once enough accrued and subsequently fell to the floor, I carefully picked the pieces up and placed them back in the pile on the desk; I am obsessive enough to not allow debris on my floor but not disciplined enough, perhaps, not to keep these pencil shavings on the desk, because I am silly enough to think that doing so makes me more like writers (a writer, one writer) from the 1920s. But I'm not honest enough to say it is silly. So I attempt to fabricate or live a life of a person an ocean away and a whole person's lifetime past.

The back stairwell of the apartment building overlooks an alley loomed over by a children's park and another apartment building. To smoke, I lean with my elbows on the dusty railing of the landing between the third and second stories. When a train rattles several blocks away, I crane my head to the left to see it pass; when I hear children scream or laugh, to the right. But mostly I am here at night, peering down and waiting for the rats.

I can tell you from where they come—their burrows or holes or dens or whatever rats keep. I can tell you that there are only one or two large males here, one or two large females, and a handful of young—or brood or fry or offspring or joeys or kids or whatever rats produce.

I had only ever seen one rat before living in Chicago—a *real* rat, not a field mouse. The nutrients they need are not readily available in alleyless, dumpsterless, mostly unpopulated, hilly, untrafficked, unlittered Ohio. No, but we had raccoons and opossums—animals that could tear open trash bags and closed Tupperware and lift the still-attached can lid that is pressed back into the can so that its sharp edge does not tear the thin plastic while en route to the trash can.

Rats can chew through almost anything, but rats like Chicago because they like alleys because they like dumpsters because they can be gotten into with relative ease compared to chewing through tin or plastic: more than once, one of the big males climbed a chain-link fence below to reach a low-hanging power line, traversed it maybe three or four feet, and stretched itself across the gap over to the open, blue, graffitied dumpster. I wondered, watching this, if rats have thumbs the way raccoons do, the way humans do, and unlike the vestigial bumps that squirrels do. Instead of actually checking, though, by going down into the alley to examine the cold dead one that bloodied the cement around its mouth, I assure myself they do not by laughing as they lose their balance and swing to the underside of the power line—though perhaps the fact that they still hang on is proof that they do.

I do not know if opossums have thumbs either, but I know that I once found one asleep inside an upright trash can. After the expected unhinged-mandible hiss from my waking it and the realization that removing it would be impossible, realizing its permanence, at least for the day until night fell and it continued its nocturnal roving, I named it Eliot.

Perhaps the year before, I had been taught "The Lovesong of J. Alfred Prufrock," and T.S. Eliot quickly became my favorite poet. I created indexes of him all around me for so long that I can no longer tell if I would ever think of him on my own—or if, instead, I only do because I force his proximal existence. I can't even say anymore that he is my favorite poet.

Were you to ask, I would tell you he is. Favorites become habitual; liking and disliking, a pattern. It might only be a fear of change or loss or the shock of sensation that comes with crisis, when we test our admonishments, that prevents us from moving on from these and, ultimately, being honest. But I won't do that.

He has become too much a part of my identity, and I do, in fact, fear losing him: I named the opossum Eliot as an homage to Tom, to "Old Possum"; I named my first houseplant and only fichus Neville as an homage to Virginia Woolf's character in *The Waves* whose antecedent is Lytton Strachey but whose name is so much more French and sophisticated than the character based on Eliot, Louis; the first of my published poems was printed under my initials, a way to show that I had a literary forebearer; my largest series of poems (also the only) follows a fictional Thomas Stearns, a vagrant who is very much an aspect of me; when I had a significant other named Elliott, whose favorite poem was also "Prufrock," I thought of him—or *made* myself think of him—*as* T.S. Eliot; and, later, when I wrote about him and needed to change his name, the alias seemed all too obvious.

I used to believe in metempsychosis, and then I didn't. And then I started getting in the habit of referring to my writer-friends by the names of authors of whom they or their writing reminded me. And they did the same for me.

I used to wonder if my soul was his—and if that would even be possible with the time between his death and my birth. I told people I thought I was, even though I couldn't explain how or why. And still, today, I tell people that I sometimes feel I am Eliot—even though I no longer necessarily believe in any of this (and, if I do, I know now that it must be instantaneous, unless of course it was, twice already, and there was a death in the interim)—but that I am not, in fact, T.S. Eliot.

While moving into this new apartment, a friend who was helping lug four hundred books up that back stairwell, upon first seeing the space itself, told me that this apartment suited me more than my previous, larger, newly renovated apartment. I agreed, reluctantly. When I first saw the space, I knew it was the one I would choose, because my choices had already been dwindling and my budget remained meager.

But I also chose it because it reminded me so much of how I imagined (sometimes *struggling*) authors to have lived in England in the early twentieth century. It reminded me of how I imagine Tom to have lived: cooped up in a too-small space, too busy or too genius or too poor to find something with better floors, more space, in better condition generally. I think that this is the kind of apartment graduate students ought to have: old and run-down with alcoholic neighbors, chosen in haste and out of need, out of necessity and desperation—though one may grow to say they love it and, after a year and a half, realize their error. Graduate students should *only* find apartments the week after they separate themselves from a significant other—forced to abandon a life they created with them, escaping to something else—something not necessarily altogether better but something more *them* or, if not, at least solitary.

When I came earlier that morning to have the building manager grab my keys from what would be my own kitchen cabinet, I stood in the empty space with the early morning summer light stuttering in through the blinds and onto the light wood floor and cream-colored walls, and I imagined my desk positioned to the left of that doorway to the hallway and how Tom would approve.

His desk would have been in the exact same position, and his too would be covered in burnt wick and pencil shavings that occasionally dropped to the floor. His bed could only be where I've placed my own, his kitchen table in the only place available for mine, the desk only right here.

No, furniture arrangement is neither unique nor creative; it is both dictated and limited by the space: there are only so many permutations and possibilities, and it seems there are never many. The placement of the bookshelves is inevitable; the chair's is inevitable; the desk's is inevitable. (The desk, inevitable.) Everything is patterned and repeated—and so, for how many decades—under the physics of pigeonhole principle.

I say this with no authority, of course, but I am certain that the building was built in the 1920s, and I am certain that it has yet to be remodeled: judging by the floor's disrepair, it must be original; the toilet, reminiscent of a public restroom's, with its tanklessness, must certainly be original, though the flushing apparatus itself is clearly new; I have electric floorboard heaters, but I can see where the radiators once were; the walls are cracked from stress, none of the wood fits perfectly together, the molding is more paint or caulking than wood now; the door handles are some that I have only seen in *Alice in Wonderland* and must be as original as the doors. And although my desk is, I know, a 1950s creation, it feels left-handed and as quintessentially 1920s to me as the apartment.

While I can imagine Tom living in a space such as this, I laugh at the thought of a young, recently married Jinny in such a place, even as only a guest. No, she needed a yard through which she and Tom could walk, hands in pockets, hands at sides, large noses, blurry, blurry photographs. But I do not. I do not have visitors; my friends and I see each other at school, in and between classes. We drink together—I less so than they, so I see them less, generally. But the point is that I don't invite anyone over, and no one asks to visit.

I was told long before I moved to or even visited this city that I would love it, that I belong there, here; and it only took looking at one obviously art nouveau-inspired entrance to a subway to realize how right these friends of mine had been. The entrance, with its French curves, its thick but rounded typeface—probably closest to *Paris Metro*—the very color, the only color, I associate with turn-of-the-century decorative art, that pale green of newly-oxidized copper.

I love art nouveau: the floral and feminine, the pencil-under-watercolor paired with the thick hair, all the movement, that lettering, the vectors. And there is so much of it in Chicago: that subway entrance, bar signs clearly incorporating designs of Alphonse Mucha, circular windows and swooping doorways, rust, watercolor, all of it. The Great Chicago Fire of 1871 decimated the city, and its rebuilding began right during the time that art nouveau began to appear and certainly continued after Mucha's influence became better felt. The city—whether it is in actuality or not—*is* art nouveau to me.

Eliot saw it, lived through its peak. His own art is nothing like art nouveau; he, his philosophy, was too *modern*, too twentieth century. But he, along with all those surrounding him—Stein, Picasso, Woolf, Modigliani, Joyce, Man Ray, Pound, Stravinsky, almost Fitzgerald—was a product of this art style; only *after* living through it, he fought against it, created something new. The novelty—of modernism, of art nouveau, and of Chicago, especially—always comes from the destruction of what is prior; a fire with unknown origins catches and burns for two or four days, and then, for the next decade or two, we begin again, start over, abandon what didn't work, neglect what we didn't like. Although it isn't *neglecting* as much as preparing for—*pencil-sharpening*, as it were.

No, Eliot is *not* art nouveau, but he'd have lived in a city that was, even if only to strengthen his conflagration. There is also something in him that suggests he'd never live through any slow recreation or allow pencil shavings on his desk: his poetry is too clean, the rhymes too intentional (do I dare, do I dare say *predictable*), too organized to allow such messes in his physical surroundings; in photographs, his hair is parted just so, his trousers rolled, always a tie, always svelte. He is handsome, despite his nose. And I impose this same decorum on all gay men: apartments that look like film sets; Ikea furniture, not because it lasts or is good, but because it is generally cheap for its foreignness, expensive for its quality, and that is what new homeowners are *meant* to purchase; black and white; maybe cool grays and cement; industrial and hard; leather and never woven fabric; clothes perfectly aligned and all hanging in the same direction; cleaning daily, never dirty; except the dishes, never done.

Ostentatious. Performative, all of it. This is how I stereotype the way gay men live—that is, this is how gay men are stereotyped. And I know that Tom never shared a bed with his wife, Vivienne (and of course a gay man would marry a woman named Vivienne), and he has been described as "fundamentally gay"—though I have a hard time believing it. But the fact is that it was hinted to me, long long ago, and now I use it against him—this externally made identity automatically becoming fodder for *knowledge* or imagining: he would not have lived like this; he'd have lived like *that*. And Woolf's Louis demonstrates this—this hyperawareness of self and decorum and appearance and attraction to Percival.

While I identify with him as much as I do—perhaps because of his sexuality, as the first writer I knew (or knew I knew) who shared mine—he is also an ideal for me, a kind of foil and aspiration: he is a great writer, seems to be a good friend, is cultured and well-dressed. But, also, people say he's gay, and that changes the dynamic entirely.

Perhaps, were I older, I'd have seen him give a lecture—as old as one of my oldest professors who *had* attended one of his lectures—and stopped him in the hallway afterward, complimented him on his suit (gray) or poetry (don't compliment both, and do not ask about Jinny or Vivienne), and he would take me to dinner, and we'd drink wine, and he would intimidate me so much that I would barely speak, and I would be too self-conscious to eat, and he would invite me to his hotel room, and he would smile a smug smile, and I would finally muster the courage to ask him some question that he would answer by way of undressing himself—which would be no answer at all—and he would not undress me but leave me to do it myself, as if he were above that (and he would be, wouldn't he), and he would ask me to him, and I would go to him, and he would tell me what to do, and I would do it, and, once it were done, he would leave me on the chair or floor or bed, and he would shower then quickly put on clean clothes (all gray) and make to exit and say, facing the door, that I could stay for as long as I desire, so long as I am gone before ten.

The potential for narcissism or egotism is palpable, although this desire, this fantasy, may merely be a desire to reunite with my once-body, perhaps be transferred again and back. Always osmosis. Mostly, though, we are vastly different. Oceans.

But I haven't been able to tell for a while now whether I'd prefer to be with him or be him—and desire so often confuses itself this way, mistaking *possession* for *identity*.

Those indexes shored up around me are disappearing. I have neither written nor thought about *Thomas* (except for here); I do not care what that very real man with the very real alias is doing now or if he ever loved me; I have not worried about being labeled as a *gay* writer in years; I have found a new coterie in Chicago, and, though their personalities or writing also remind me of others', we do not assign aliases; in my most recent move, Neville dried up in the heat of a car and was abandoned in one of those open, blue, graffitied dumpsters weeks later (because, although I knew he was dead, I wanted to give myself enough time to attempt revival).

Neville was replaced by a plant I call Rhoda, another character from *The Waves*. I like her, because she is melancholic, trapped, not stifled but frozen. I like her, because her words are Percy Shelley's, whose poetry I think I have always loved more, thought was more compelling and in a style I find more mature, whose life I know more about, whose relationships I find more interesting, whose sexuality I would *like* to identify with more, whom I read more often, with whom I am simply more familiar—but cannot allow myself to love even a bit more than Thomas. Even though I honestly might.

So why didn't I save myself for Percy, and why do we ever feel the need to commit by proxy. Why did I force myself to love Tom only for loving Jinny, wanting to be like her by loving like her. Why Percy for the sake of Mary.

Because that's how love works. We substitute to make our circumstances feel more manageable. Everything is placeholder, and everything holds a place, because desire may never expend itself; instead, we exhaust and exchange. There is a void to fill, a pot to plant again. These are shallow graves we cover. Both when we move and when we move on, we hold the two blue-prints printed on tracing paper atop one another and hold them to the sun, determining what stays right where it is and what must move, out of necessity.

How Not to Drown

I have a desk again: a 1950s spindly legged, two-wide-and-one-tall-drawered, worn, sighing, coffee cup-ringed, likely easily breakable Eames-style writing desk.

I am a writer, I tell myself, *so I need a desk*. I thought for several weeks that not having one was the reason I didn't write, but not writing and not having a desk have had little to do with each other. I had been reading Nicole Krauss's *Great House*, at the center of which is a massive thousand-drawered desk; the constant attention and focus on the importance of such a piece of furniture undoubtedly made me desire one. We desire that which we do not have. (This is Lacanian.)

It belonged to a Chilean poet, and one of the narrators of the book had difficulty writing anywhere but at it. Three writers possessed the desk, and it seemed to grant each extraordinary talent: from within the hundred drawers, there seeped a certain gift. The desk affords them creativity and purpose, which I feel I have been lacking, as I have written next to nothing for over two months: I have sat down a few times to write and have created brief outlines or sentences that I cannot seem to part with that have sprouted out of me while doing dishes.

There was a single locked drawer in that billion-drawered tank of a desk, positioned at each of the four hearts of *Great House*. I know what the owners of the desk received, I know how they metabolized it; but I do not know if it leaked from the desk itself, evaporated from its porous surfaces, or if whatever it was came from that single drawer, that single, locked drawer. That keyhole, that way to view those things we miss, we have missed, that run away from us, that escape us with a phrase, that we chase, that have been taken away from us, that are not here but *there*. I wonder if, were I in that particular fiction, I would have spoken to it and what I could have gotten from it or if the characters *did* bend down, their lips almost pressed to the silver panel around the hole, and whispered something, something warmed by their throat but chilled as it passed through the crying gate.

Not one of my desk drawers locks, but I have gotten something from this desk nonetheless. *Something*, I tell myself, has percolated out. And I am beginning to wonder what else I could get or find if I found a certain special keyhole to speak to. There is the one for my bathroom door, at which I stare as I sit on the toilet. It reminds me of the one to whom Alice spoke: tall and narrow, with two flat-head screw eyes, a bulbous knob nose, that pliable, stretching, gaping mouth. I tried to look through that hole once, but the way is blocked. Every time I sit and stare at it, I think about crying and having it tell me what to do, what to eat, and how much, how not to drown; I want to look through it, to see if I can spot my quarry. And now, I want to fold myself over and tell it something so quietly that no one else could hear me: I want to pray through it.

But I don't know how. So I don't. Because I cannot find the divinity in a keyhole. Naturally, only a keyhole would do—not a window, not an archway of any kind, nothing made of brick, not a mouth, no human orifices, not the mouth of a cave, nothing in a church, nothing underground, not a revolving door, although maybe. Perhaps they are all divine, and I just haven't seen it.

It has been that I wake up late, and I do not write. I exercise, then I do not write. After I read, I do not write—not anymore, not during these past two months. I sleep, then I drink coffee. I do dishes, I dust, I vacuum. I send emails, and I check the mail; I make phone calls, and I purchase milk. I take out the garbage. But because I am not lacking time, I have no need to keep track of it and thus can never recall exactly how my time was spent. *For how long did I sit drinking coffee this morning. What did I do while drinking it. Were the dishes done before or after I dirtied more.* Of course it only matters because I am asked to—to account for my day, my time alone.

I attempt to make up for my perceived indulgences by allowing us, encouraging us, to do exactly what *he* wants to do—even if I *do* want to write. I've been asked to believe compromise and sacrifice are necessary for cohabitation. Not that it matters much: I have never been able to write near others. It is an overwhelming empathy, I tell myself, a kind of Angel in the House: *You are ignoring them. They know what you are doing, and it is self-indulgent. It is verging on hedonism. It is selfish. And you know they feel this way, and you feign being unapologetic. But you wish to apologize. I wish to apologize. Apologize to them. Stop typing. Stop thinking about the previous sentence and the one that will follow; stop thinking about how this will fit in your collected works, about your biographer. Writing is secondary to everything. Tertiary. Last. You have responsibilities to these people. What are they doing. If they are laughing, is it about you. At what are they looking. Do they refuse to make eye contact with you. What was that sound. You had better check. You need to check. Stop writing and check. Stop writing.*

When I first moved with the desk, I had to pack carefully, concisely, tightly, because I was too cheap to buy new boxes, but rather used old ones and bags. But even still, I could not find a place for all my books: I postponed packing them by counting them. Hundreds of books to arrange by importance, then by binding, then by size; then to stack in boxes and slip into bags. Packing them, I felt guilty knowing that it would be two of my friends who would carry these boxes into the moving truck and from it up a flight of stairs to my new apartment. Why couldn't I have gotten rid of some. Shouldn't I have. But I felt worse when I could not find a place for the last two shelves' worth.

As soon as I knew the move was impending, I fought the urge to destroy everything—drown everything in the lake and compose a new life with only my chair and my clothes. Realistically, my books would have been spared; but in that moment, I wanted to destroy them, burn them. I doubted then (as I do now) that I would even notice their absence, not only because I would be surrounded by so much change but also because they were the smallest, the least important and likely unread. Conflagration would not have been generative.

So I removed the drawers of my desk, carried them to my bookshelf, and I loaded them with those last shelves before replacing the drawers and taping them closed. And that simply, my new desk, the one I carried a third of the way across Lincoln Park, became no more than a storage unit. And I felt regret.

The talent of the authors in *Great House* was seemingly multiplied by that desk in a way other than affording personal inspiration, as any one object might. But writing desks do not help a person to write in any way other than the physical. Desks are not imbued with powers; magic is not real; inanimate objects do not collect exerted talent or skill from previous locales or owners the way they collect dust or injuries; they do not breathe; there are no accumulations of spirits, no density of souls; one never occupies the same physical space as a ghost; desks are not mythical.

But I had hoped mine would be. My desk—as old and as used as it is, with its nicked corners and countless water rings, its top surface feeling much like sandstone or limestone or something finely riveled, stroked by how many fingertips (as finely riveled) in the past sixty years—must contain a piece of somebody, pieces of some bodies. It is sitting there, exhaling something, slowly giving itself off, exhausting itself, permeating the air; that is certainly why it is so textured: it has given away parts of itself to the air, and, once given, it cannot replace.

The desk *is* like a fingertip: I learned that when one stays in water, the *pruniness* of one's fingers is caused by water absorption, though I think this has actually been disproven. When I was very young, I was certain that it was caused by the exact opposite: we are so much water, and when we stay in water for too long, our fingers and toes wrinkle; I thought something had been taken away, because we are water, and water is able to escape to be with more water, a great consciousness of water. Osmosis. The desk has done the same thing, only instead of water, the spirits or souls or magic in it have an air-like property, and thus they are escaping all the time, creating depressions, dips, a riveled texture by way of long, dry sighs of energy and faith and crisis. I live with ghosts and foreign bodies I cannot put away or destroy. I inhale it, the body, the argon; it seeps into my pores, it penetrates me, the keratin; it lives with me, but I try and cannot avoid it.

I am more than *I*, now, more than it too. I have become part of an equation: I am the relationship, now; I am air too.

Carrion

I do not remember much from my mornings. Each, an echo of the previous: sometimes delayed, sometimes incomplete, but the same sounds, the same motions. The apartment is a misty-tan and blurry; I make coffee, and I roll cigarettes; he takes out the dog, I make her breakfast; I pull down two white ceramic mugs from the shelf, spoon two spoons of sugar in one, one in the other, and some milk in both; we pour coffee, I stir both mugs, he stirs his again, and we step out to smoke.

Two mornings ago, we had the luxury of waking up after the sun: delayed. I have always felt lucky to have our smoking stoop—the stair landing overlooking a gated alley between buildings. The birds nest here. They fly in, and they fly out, swooping between woodwork and metal. Swooping low and close, open-winged, unflapping. They perch, and they sing so often, though not songs I have learned: I know the cardinal, and I know the robin, but these are unidentified wrens and black birds (they are starlings)—songs I did not hear in my part of Ohio. I hear one begin its song, and I turn to locate it, coffee in hands, cigarette between fingers. Glasses sometimes on, sometimes off.

But lately there have also been the sudden cries of young. In an electrical box on the adjacent building, one of those black birds, which are not really black, but blue and green and with such yellow beaks, has a nest, and that nest has young. I hear them when food is brought to them.

And it dawned on me: *This has been going on for months.* I don't know the average nest-life of birds, but I had assumed it wasn't long. Maybe six weeks, I don't know. However long, this nest kept its young for longer. I imagined them, briefly: pale-feathered, mottled- and dirty-feathered, weak-limbed, big empty-eyed morlocks—all deformity and sunlessness.

I said, *Those babies*—aware of my anthropomorphization— *Those babies have been in that nest for too long.* (It is unnatural to harbor something for so long, to refuse to expose it to anything other than your self, to guard something so closely. It is wrong to insist on proximity, on shared life, of commitment and union. Perhaps. Perhaps selfish to shelter and paranoid to barricade.)

That evening, I went to open that tall black not-wrought-iron gate for him. I walked down the steps, rain-warped, stained too-brown, no knots, no grain, and I walked our gray sidewalk, which is not as much on the side of anything as it is *between.* It is a walkway, and *side* is perhaps merely short for *cement.* Regardless, I walked it, and I looked at the ground, for I have recently again taken up the habit of avoiding stepping on cracks. If the toe of my shoe, where my toes do not sit, touches it—if that gap between heel and ball falls over it; if I kick it—if I step right on it.

As I watched my shoes—or maybe I didn't have shoes on at all—I saw something small and blue and pink and skeletal. A *baby.* Fallen and cracked open, featherless, eyeless. Only as deformed as I had imagined, but differently.

My immediate thought was that I should not have said what I had—that I pressured the universe to push them out. I felt guilty, not in that I had any direct influence, for I know that even if they heard me, my language is not theirs and so could not have understood me. I felt guilty in a cosmic, karmic way. That kind when you wish someone were dead and then he dies.

I did not know how long before starlings ordinarily left the nest, but now I do: there is no set time. One may fledge the night after it hatches, or fledgling may coincide with migration. It doesn't matter.

And I like that word, *fledge. To fledge.* To develop feathers and muscles for flight; to cover something with or something like feathers; to attach feathers to an arrow; to rear until ready to depart.

He tried to console me, suggesting that perhaps it tried to fly too soon. As if there is comfort there. There is not, because I was suggesting they should have flown already. But I was wrong. This was proof that I was wrong: if they were ready to leave, to fly, this would not have looked like a ghost-deer, a cow fetus; it would not have been naked against cement—perhaps against cement, still, but not with bare flesh.

The fact is that this fledgling—this attempted fledgling—was incomplete. It had not a single feather, just that wrinkled thin transparent and blue flesh covering hollow bones and barely covering veins and intestines, the dark gray-blue of eyeballs behind unopened lids. And there is something fascinating about being able to see inside of ourselves, isn't there. To be able to count our veins, locate our heart, try to map intestines. It is mesmerizing to unnecessarily make sure that we are whole and complete—

the relief to find we have ten fingers and ten toes and only two eyes, only one nose and let us count our teeth—but we can lose these and lack these and replace these or not without being incomplete, as they exist within a range. Like bones.

I knew that what he said was not the case: we do not attempt flight until after we have the wings and muscles, until after we coat ourselves with molasses and shower ourselves with down.

Carrion

It is raven season again. I have felt cold, and I have felt lonely. I have been lazy, and I have been thinking about ambitions, love, travel, and how the body clings to another season. I have been wondering if we could ever have the power to say *no* to something, ever have the foresight to deny the next thing; if we ever have the agency to remove ourselves from the serial. Of course we cannot skip a season, but we might not embrace it as ardently, knowing that eventually, in the cycle, we would come across something that we *do* like and wish to embrace.

But. One part of me assumes today will be just like yesterday, and the other part of me accepts each day and each season as its own: I cannot hold out for fall, because it is summer, and I have to live through it; I should not wish today is warm just because yesterday was cold, because today *is* cold, and no wishing, no anticipating will change that. I am singular and constantly in a single moment, assuming winter will last forever, as will spring and summer and fall. But seasons do not last.

Ravens like the disinterring and the melting and that perception of *new*. They like the new warmth and ruffle against the new cold. They do not migrate but, rather, tolerate the change. This is their home, so they stay, and they wait.

Of course, there are no ravens here. The large black birds roosting in the bare tree outside my window are not ravens. But

I will always call these days of melting snow coming twice every year—during warm early-winter days and again at the advent of spring—*raven season*: there is poetry there that does not exist in referring to it as *crow season* or *the weather pattern marked by my noticing the crows outside my window.*

It's just this: I am confused at the same time as the weather seems to be, which happens to be the same time that I notice them. I create the term *raven season*, because I try to convince myself that *everyone* is confused, not just me. And this is only indicative of my current depression: raven season is chemical, circumstantial, and biological. It is a way to provide patch or ointment, to stop the itch, the watering eyes.

A dream I had only last night helped me realize that raven season is related not to weather but to unrest, uncertainty and questioning, exploration, and desiring simple, uninhibited truths (each raven, all confusion, I thought, would have disappeared had I simply heard *I love you* or *yes* or *forever*—or *I don't* or *no* or *never*):

They are many, and they are intolerably close to me. They are threatening. I am trying to move past their barricade. I feel the cool oily edge of their beaks snapping at my fingers and ears, and I use my broader palms to spread their darkened, violent maxillary and mandibular rostrums, those well-formed growths of keratin. I am afraid they are going to begin cawing in my ear, deafening me. I am trying to hold them away. I do not want to be confused, I do not want to wait for answers. I want to be beyond transition.

These bouts of confusion and dislodgement, of excess desiring—which is also to say *ravens* and *this season I have come to describe as theirs*—have always reminded me of raccoons with their greasy palms and arched backs, their black eyes, their sexual noises and posturing, ducking between trashcans after breakups at night; of the hunting I have done, the quarry-chasing and quarry-digging; of a youth spent drinking vodka out of plastic cups and staying up until it is too cold to go outside, but going out anyway to smoke; of pounds of books I love the most and carry with me; of suicide attempts; and of the sudden longing I sometimes experience for Rust Belt cities slowly ascending mountainsides or the clear-skyed-snowing of Utah.

But this would make more sense: carrion, fruit pressed between fingers, against palm and against hardwood flooring, excrement, death. The season delivers ghosts to the forefront of my consciousness: after things are hidden, even with the lightest of coverings of transitional snows, or the lifting of such a veil, I am given something seemingly new, a way to start again on those things I have fucked up, or a way to abandon them for something new. To begin again is a blessing and a horror: you start over with the same questions and fears as before, you again travel through a narrow battlefield with scavengers who beg for the dead. The snow and ice always melt, and not only do the birds come to eat those things that have suffocated and been pressed under the weight of the cold but also the memories of those dead are raised as ghosts, definitely there but with infinitely less substance. Things melt, things change, there is transition, and I remember. And for a while, until the heat or cold has set in for the following months, until the depression lifts, until I am no longer scared to be bitten by large horrible dream-ravens. I have to live alongside them. I have to live along-side not knowing what I can say when, not knowing who is when, not knowing.

There are two ravens always with Odin, except at dawn, when Huginn and Muninn fly from his shoulders, spread their greasy wings against the wind, and circle themselves effortlessly around the world. It is only then, maybe, that he questions, that he is uncertain, anticipating either abandonment or absolute devotion.

But by breakfast, both return to his shoulders and whisper to him all the information they gathered in their travels. Odin is blind, but he sees through his ravens, through Huginn and Muninn, whose names translate to *Thought* and *Memory*. Because he is blind—or because he is missing an eye—he is dependent on them to see anything, to see the world, to see everything. At all.

They are free to fly, and so why should they return. He owns them, and they are obligated to, I suppose; but is their loyalty purely mythological, metaphysical. Do they stay only because Odin is a god and has power over them. If they could choose differently, would they. If Odin were less respectable, like Thor or Zeus even, would they risk punishment or dis-existence not to return, to be free of him and perhaps each other. Is it fear.

Fear could keep them: fear of dis-existence, of sudden unma-teriality. Fear of anger and potential punishment. Fear of not knowing what else to do, what else they *could* do. Fear of not knowing who or what they are without him. Fear that they only *are* with him.

These two birds have been on my mind for years. They were the first I knew of ravens, and, because we so often evaluate new experiences based on what we know of old experiences—how significant others are always better or worse than, we know how a person will treat us because we expect to be treated similarly by similar people—and because the mythology functions as a series of metaphors, the constitution of all ravens I have experienced has been affected: they always whisper to the blind, describe the world for those who cannot see. Ravens are always thought, and they are always memory: they exist on shoulders, snapping beaks near ears.

I call crows *ravens*, because I want ravens. And because no black corvids are so dissimilar from each other. I want the world imagined for me. I want it determined for me, made predictable and described for me, definitively, without doubt. I want full and complete trust. And loyalty. So I make it up: they are saying something, and I really want to know what; I want to know *to what* they think I am blind. I want to understand my own metaphor.

I don't even actually know that Odin is blind. What I do know, as much as one can *know* a myth, is that he only has one eye, that he placed the other in Mimir for a drink of its wisdom-filled water at the roots of the world tree. Missing an eye does not mean blindness, though; and, having drunk from that water, he should know everything already and need neither Huginn nor Muninn. Odin should not need his ravens to see for him.

They aren't said to help him travel, do not seem to direct him as if he were blind like a dog. Perhaps they are interpreting what is in front of him. Of course, there is the possibility that ravens are such good communicators and he is so attuned to them that there is the illusion of not being blind despite being so—blinded from another story, *not* from having placed an eye in a well. But Odin is not omnipresent; neither are they, but they are two, and they can fly, and they travel more quickly. In this sense, Huginn and Muninn are not responsible for telling him everything (or anything) but merely for describing what is happening outside of his knowledge of everything, about the *changing* things.

This is what ravens are. They are two; they are depth perception. They are eyes, and they are braille.

They are carrion-feeders—they live off the dead. And Huginn and Muninn are ghosts, and ghosts were only once alive. And Odin hanged himself from Yggdrasil. And Yggdrasil is ash. And *ash* meant *spear*, and Odin used his to pierce himself in the side when he hanged from the tree. And ash is to ash, I hear. And ash is the product of conflagration—and it all simply points toward death, toward dying, that thing we, as a culture, already know about ravens.

But this feels too simple for me: these ravens are mine, and they should not have to mean what everyone seems to think they mean. Huginn and Muninn may be symbols, but the ravens outside my window are *mine*. I have known them as death-messengers for too long. Ravens are more than birds of blood, or they should be. Somehow. They are indexes of crumbling and of change.

I can make them more than this too.

Ravens can be metaphors for anything: I graft my own meaning to them, stitching what I think I need to them so that when I see them, they return that thing to me. They are *I love you* and they are *I never have* and *never will* and *always* and *stay* and *move in* and *yes* and *now* and *don't you see* and—. But, ultimately, my ravens are certainly not here to tell me of my mortality, because that is not only simple but also inefficient: I take a pill every day that tells me I am mortal, and I have a tattoo—which I know I have every day, though I do not necessarily *see* it—which verbally indicates the glory of my being here. Ravens are something else, because I do not need them to be that.

(Freud: my certainty here may only indicate that that is *exactly* what they are. I have no choice but to admit that possibility. In a way, in one way, they *are* still death, dying, my mortality. But death is not so different from change, and dying is not so different from transition, and how often are we burned after death. So I admit the possibility. And I continue to negate. Because I want them to be signs of definitive answers.)

I watch recordings of and read texts about object-retrieval tests. I am panicked by non-humans possessing logic and reason and meta-tool-use so similar to and perhaps surpassing us and ours. The large black bird hops and slides across a metal table and picks up a thin brown stick between rostrums; it uses this stick to pull a longer stick to the front of a barred box with quick, rickety, ticking head movements that seem so deft; it drops the short stick and inserts its pointed, dynamic keratin protrusion between the bars to retrieve the previously inaccessible longer stick, then hops and slides over to yet another box and uses this stick to pull the food within reach. Then snaps it up, disappearing in its violent maw.

I have seen this so many times, with different birds, in different locations, each with a slight variation. I watch their bodies, count their toes, try to distinguish single feathers from the flat black robes that cover them, but my fascination is with how their bodies enact what I perceive to be their thought, how a body itself is merely a tool; I pause the videos at the moment just after the bird realizes it cannot reach the food with only its beak. Pause again when, I presume, its eye lands on the first stick. There is a head-tilt or a turn of the head to focus another eye on the same thing or to look at something else or see more. I try to look beyond the cornea for thought, to understand what is happening in that small brain.

Birds adapt. Birds learn. They learn rush hour, learn traffic patterns determined by stoplights, learn how frequently trash day comes. They are not completely reactionary, the way we often think of animals; these birds predict: weather, dangers.

Corvids recognize and remember faces and schedules. (I wish I could see them seeing me.) This is comforting—something (some things) knows me and can show me aspects of myself that I did not see; some things (something) know others and can tell me things about them that I do not know, cannot see. They travel and report. Whisper in my ear. They travel, observe, learn, recognize, then return to me.

Ancestors taught their young to recognize faces, communicate descriptions of them. They pass knowledge of any physical thing, anything that can be described, through their generations. Crows, like rooks, are avid storytellers—but, unlike how it is for rooks, who kill each other over bad stories, for crows, there is no such thing. All stories are valuable. So I wonder if this is what they are trying to tell me, to teach me—if I am like one of their young, and they are telling me with their quiet, soothing familial dialect (it sounds so much like cooing) who is going to hurt me or break me or feed me or kill me, if they are trying to tell me how to pass all my knowledge on to the young I do not possess. Or if instead they recognize something in my face, if I am food or danger to them, if I possess one of those faces about which their young are told.

I look at them, because I want to see them recognizing me, remembering, though we are not *recognized* as much as *differentiated from* or *compared to*.

But really, when I think about what ravens see in my face, I am wondering if I look like Odin. If corvids are able to pass such information through generations, then certainly the ones I see would remember or still see Odin's one eye, his hood or hat or staff, his reddened restricted neck; they would remember or still feel the bulk or slightness of his shoulders through the leather he wore. Perhaps he perpetually had stubble on his cheeks, the way I do; perhaps they understand these things over my eyes to be proof of blindness; perhaps his and my skin tones are identical, and we are the same height and have the same narrow gait, the same cat's eye ring on right middle finger.

There must be something about me that registers as *Odin*

to them, as they are following me and trying to tell me something—or perhaps not *something* as much as *everything*. But they aren't telling me anything, as they are not speaking to me; rather, I know I am making them, and myself, into something we are not. I am making myself a god so that I feel important, making myself a god with *thought* and *memory* as messengers, so that I have companions because I feel alone. So that I feel certain, because I am confused.

Carrion

I have come to the realization that they are *of course*. And I hate that idiom—*of course*. I do not often hear it used in any sense but to assert that something should not be argued. It is used as validation. Something is *of the ordinary course of events*. That is, they are predictable in navigation. *This* course, *this* track, *this* race. They are more predictably *here* than *there*, *here* than *elsewhere*. To say *they are of course* suggests only that they exist, that, in life, in the world, *of course* I would happen upon them. This is possibility, not probability, though. They actually are not *of course*, not here. They actually do *not* exist here. They could. It is possible. So my saying that they are, for me, *of course*, is problematic.

Ravens exist.

Of course.

But *course* is also agreement (not entirely different): to say something is *of course* is not only to say that the something is inarguable but also that you agree, that you are of the same opinion, are looking at the same evidence and drawing the same conclusion. *Of course ravens exist. Ravens exist, of course.* And *course* is many things. *To course* is to hunt, chase, pursue; it is to run through; it is, in a way, to look for.

But to then say that ravens are *of course* in one sense becomes a lie: I don't *course* ravens; I happen upon them. There is something fleeting in the idiom, too, which I like: as we stumble upon them, they are running through billions of lives, to make their appearance. They are daily traversing the globe. We never see them for long. They are looking for newly dried land, and they are gathering all information.

It was strange to see them both at the same time—both ravens, the two that make quick stops everywhere before going everywhere else, strange that they traveled together this time. Of course, it is only strange because they have never looked as if a vast net had been cast up into the air; which, after a few moments would sink slowly down upon the trees until every twig seemed to have a knot at the end of it. Instead, two seems to be the number. The maximum. The exception, really. Most often, one, solitary.

He and I were talking on the back stairs when I noticed them. They were on the chimney of the building across the alley and to our right, a floor and a roof and a chimney's height above where we were sitting. I noticed them, saw them, looked at. I watched as they flew in together and buffeted their wings against the wind only once before landing. Because they were not there before, because we did not stumble upon them, and because they stopped within eyesight, it was like a visitation. And I thought, *of course.*

Of course I would notice them, and *of course he* would not; *of course* when I heard the sound of their wings slicing the ridges and ripples and roughness of the air, I was able to identify them, without seeing them (because they are predictable); *of course* there were two. And *of course* they were private, for he did not ask me what had taken my attention away from him, if only briefly (if only visually). That may be because we were arguing, were angry and yelling and I probably had tears welling up and my looking away from him would be expected. Of course. It is hard to look at him when he makes me cry.

I thought *of course* because I am no longer alarmed by them as I had been before, by their huge and haunting (and I hate that word) and ancient and disgusting corporeality. Because I did not find them comforting, did not need them to translate for me, did not need them to deliver his message. For he was there with me, mad at me, for something. They are no longer my only company, because now I have him. That is, I thought of them as being of the ordinary course of events because they had suddenly become ordinary, nothing other than themselves.

He has been teaching me how to accept things as they are, just as my mother has been telling me since I was very young—telling me that I overanalyze, that I think too much, that I expect things to have direct paths and connections to the universal, the most deeply hidden, the uncovered aspects of the human. Which is to say, they felt *of course* because they were not entirely unexpected.

They are identified and labeled and charted and can be found on maps and there are words to describe them and name them and differentiate them, and we know their stories and all the things they represent, for what they are metaphor. But perhaps they are never truly *expected*. Existence does not necessitate presence. Not in my course. Not in our course. But the raven is myth to me; crows, metaphors for a metaphor. Ravens only exist. Of course.

I experience them differently than you. (Don't I.) The crow, the raven—it exists in all our courses, but they exist differently for me. Just as the ocean does: I know it is there, somewhere, but it is imaginary to me. Japan, the same. I have an Alphonse Mucha painting tattooed on my side, but the referent is even less real than these birds, as I got a tattoo of a print of a draft of the painting by Mucha. I love him, but I do not know him, have never experienced him, do not *know* him. He is *of course*, but this only means that he is, to me, possible. That is, what we do not experience, we cannot *know*. We cannot say to something we have not yet experienced, *of course*.

But the ocean is real to him. We talked about it. He lived there. He fled there, and he fled from there. I imagine that he saw it daily. I do not know how close he lived to it, but I imagine that one is perpetually close to water when one lives on a peninsula. I imagine. *Of course*. He tells me that the lake—our lake, here—is better than the ocean, that ocean, there. This is better: our artificial beach (because ours is artificial, I am told, not real; the natural form would be rocky and unusable) that, in parts, in our part, our private part, it mimics the natural. But it was all profit.

I envy that he can make the comparison at all.

I want to see the ocean still.

What I am trying to say is that I notice them, and others seem not to. But, moreover, I notice that I notice them and others seem not to.

No-One Suspects Your
Shoulder Blades of Wings

My experience with the sun has always lacked proximity. Often, and for years, I have been outside of it, avoiding heat and sweat. As a child, though, I was always outside, always in the heat, but that was under trees (always trees). There were, however, annual trips to the lake with my dad to be with his family, but I spent less time at the beach than I did at the Formica table on that blue, creaking, perpetually sandy floor—no matter how much time we spent with our feet under the hose. But I remember summers as a constant, insignificant peel of flesh from face and arms. Then it stopped, for years.

The pattern—or lack of anything to create a pattern—broke: I lasted more than a decade without a sunburn, severe or otherwise. Adulthood kept me inside, and socialization happened under new, larger trees. Then I got two terrible sunburns in a row: last year, from lying on the beach, my entire back red and brown and so intolerably itchy; this year, from a parade, my shoulders and biceps and forearms the painful brunt.

When we speak of Icarus in our collective tongue, we say, *He flew too close to the sun* as a means of conveying that he flew too high. While the statement is true, by measurement, it also gives a false sense of proximity: When we say, *He flew too close to the sun*, the sun becomes tangible and very close, the distance between it and the earth, it and us, becomes truncated. I prefer it that way, nonetheless, because I like to imagine his experiencing the heat, the burn, the possible combustion—of both compounds in the sun and of his layers of skin—and because heat does seem very immediate, large and looming, and tangible. There is something pleasing about conflating him with the Phoenix: the burning wings, entities of all fire, human-avian hybrid, and *meant* to die. But instead I fixate on the image of his extended arms swinging centripetal in the upswept down, circling the way light things do in alcoves (a labyrinth all of these), his laughter warmed by the sun on his naked back and escaping through a soft-lipped smile, the rachis and afterfeather sticking to his sweaty outstretched forearms, those fine hairs there—his father perhaps watching (perhaps with irritation) through eyes turned up from creation. The juvenile and quotidian complement the ingenuity and novelty of the wings fashioned by his father: the story (whether it is Icarus's or Daedalus's) feels complete and full and round, running every gamut, and reaching wide and real—sky to water, useless organics to failing mechanics, eighteen kinds of happiness, and many separate disappointments.

But at that height to which Icarus flew, when the sun is so close to the earth: I like to imagine not only the wax melting from the boy's wings, dropping the feathers so much more slowly than his non-hollow bones, but also the remaining feathers burning along with the frame and his flesh—his hair a sudden rank plume. I like to imagine the fall with his flesh charred, very much like a tomato, blackened and cracked yet so ripe underneath. His lips split and peeled back to reveal that smile again, skeletal. How he would anticipate the water below to be relief.

Reaching that height would have been not only arduous but also simply, excruciatingly painful. Had he flown high enough to melt his wings, his existence beyond the ozone would expose him to a greater than 82 percent increase in UV radiation, rupturing DNA in, I imagine, half the time (I imagine with twice the severity, as if DNA may become by degrees less recognizable). That is, even before his wings decayed, his skin would become hot cracks of lineate slate.

Peeling begins abruptly, all at once. As our bodies attempt to eject the dead and irreparably damaged cells, some areas seem to be so burnt that the skin is hard, sore, too thick and scablike to easily slip off. I see that I should not, but I cannot stop: I remember hearing that one should not pick off the skin, and, as I do, I consider the newly disclosed flesh—adolescent and not yet ready for exposure.

The picking and peeling is compulsory, anticipating the excitement and sense of achievement accompanied by the removal of not just a chip or flake but a *sheet* of skin—sometimes larger than the pad of my thumb. It attests, somehow, to the degree of damage. As if size can judge.

Last year, as I peeled, so too did he. It did not take long before we recognized our burns, but the itch settled much sooner. This was what we learned to call *Hell's itch*, something I thought his hypochondria had invented (a thought corroborated by its inexistence in any kind of medical dictionary or journal I could find). It was an itch the like of which I had experienced only once before, when I had shingles: a deep nerve-itch, one so severe that I scratched until I drew blood, an itch that makes your flesh seem parasitic. I wanted to slip it off, all of it: scratch my back with a knife, because it seemed as though the only way to get rid of it was to get rid of the skin and let the itch come out with the blood.

We gingerly massaged peppermint oil (which is the only cure for this) into each other's backs. This became a ritual, timed and scheduled so that we would not have to suffer again once its effect wore off. My itch was delayed, and it lasted longer than his. And the last time he rubbed the oil on my back was just after I had gotten out of the shower, and the water that pressed on my skin exacerbated the prickle. My flesh, though, was open, all laceration. I tolerated the pain for as long as I could (which was not long at all) until my voice became frightened and unfamiliar, cracked, and my entire body shook. He told me to get back under the water to wash off the oil, the peppermint, so I did, but the pressure hurt, the water hurt, the coldness of the peppermint hurt and crawled along my ribs and spine—*through* them, it seemed. He turned off the water (because, despite the pain, I was unable to move) and wrapped a towel around my shoulders, and I cried loudly and without pause. I could do nothing but weep, kneeling there in the shower, hands clutching at my face while he stood behind me pressing the towel into my freezing burnt skin.

That is the pain I imagine Icarus to have suffered—the crippling, debilitating, panic-inducing sensation of your skin overflowing with a pain that seems liquid in how it courses and permeates and steeps even ribcage. And how the water would in fact not be any kind of relief, despite its slap. And the fear created by the knowledge that, no matter how close he is, no matter what he is willing to do for you, you are suffering alone, and he cannot save you.

Once we began to slough, we peeled the parchment from off each other's backs, handing these bits of text to the other, who then balled it all up between thumb and finger. That, I think, was our last intimate moment—one of our last most intimate moments: calmly speaking myth behind the other's ears as our fingers felt along vertebrae and scapula (*no-one suspects your shoulder blades of wings*).

Twisting my neck and wrists now to get at the dog-ears of flesh should be cathartic—simultaneously removing something physical that has become other (because now lifeless and genetically unrecognizable) and removing something emotional that became toxic (because other and unsustainable). I think that the parallel is obvious enough for these to be conflated: each square inch removed ought to be less of him with which to live.

But this is not true beyond the fact that I think about thinking about it—the way thinking about the thought of suicide does not constitute suicidal ideation (my therapist confirms this). Instead, as I scratch and pick and pull, I am almost horrified that he and I did this for each other (*for*, as if *favor*; as if needed; as if in some way generous) and more horrified that this sunburn, a year later, reminds me of *us*, a year ago. Because I think that one should be able to will himself into unremembering. Because it is frightening, the damage that can be dealt by an object so far away—or so long ago.

There is a problem in the narrative, though, because, if the wax were to melt, and it wasn't melting already in the labyrinth, Icarus would have flown higher than the aurora—and then fallen back through it. The temperature decreases up to about 10 kilometers and then increases only to about 80 percent of sea level's temperature at 50 kilometers. This pattern of rising and dropping temperatures continues and does not reach even sea level's temperature again until an altitude of about 120 kilometers—and then he would have had to have flown higher still, because the temperature of the flat sea and the flat land I imagine the labyrinth to be on is not enough to melt beeswax.

And Icarus would have suffocated 110 kilometers lower. It would not have been even remotely—not even miraculously, not mythically—possible for Icarus to have made it high enough to melt his wax. But. If he had, there would be no body left to bury—so frozen then chipped then burnt then sublimated upon reentry.

And to say that the height physically could not be reached—because of oxygen deprivation, because of chill, because of pressure and tired muscles and someone not wanting it—is both explanation and consolation for not ever figuratively reaching that height of jubilation myself.

I consider the presumed sweetness of our gestures, our symbiotic nature present in removing our dead selves from each other. To do something for someone for yourself. It is outrage, then, at our selfishness, our codependence, and our—what—*need* to *need*. Each other. The other. This is how quickly the masochism of damaging my own flesh turns to flagellation, to punishment—picking, now, because I am angry.

But the word that strikes me regarding this moment (and it is a strike—sudden, surprising, forcing unbalance) as being most appropriate for what my burnt skin makes me feel is *disgust*: at my newly mottled skin, how different it is; at the thickness of it and how completely I am covered by it, weighing down on my shoulders very literally though not very noticeably; at the time spent picking and picking; and at how I let it all fall to the sink basin; and at how I leave it there, dark brown splinters and sheathes of radiation collecting and sticking to the porcelain. And ultimately disgust that I would ever let myself think that this had anything to do with him or with us. Despite the analogue, the fact is that these burns happened independently of each other.

Of course I consider, though, that my disgust at letting myself think of being reminded of him is proof that I do, in fact, think of him—despite how much I wish to no longer. I want a sunburn to be emotionally benign. I am tired, I think, of finding remnants of him. And of us.

Regardless (that word that appears so often when I intellectualize (mythologize)), I am more than covered in remnants of him; more than just the topmost layer of me acts as an index. Despite the (corporeal and temporal) distance between us, I am apparently meant to feel him beside me, even if only as absence: the question, *Why did he let go of your neck*, asks me to be responsible somehow, forces me into accountability; when someone apologizes for calling him handsome, there is the presumed allegiance and betrayal; the missing door, the broken door, the broken coffee pot, the only-four forks; and when I am told not to write about him, he is made a void into which I may not trespass, because the cordons are so real. His entire being is here, still here, in very close and very literal proximity.

I resist the interpretation of the myth as an allegory of youth's perceived immortality. For that to be a dominant meaning, we would need Icarus to fly, as it were, in the face of Daedalus's warning—some action to demonstrate disbelief. But this interpretation cannot even be covert, as the warning was not even of death. Mortality and immortality (or proof of either) were never mentioned. The *warning*, as we say in our collective tongue, was actually *advice: Stay the middle course*. No *or else*, not from Daedalus and never reaching Icarus's ears.

All with which we have to work is youth and joy, which notoriously make us reckless, but neither suicidal nor innately disbelieving of our mortality. I consider Icarus's jubilation at his fledge: I don't know how many would blame him for enjoying what he could, when he could—excitement from freedom, success, and flight. Why not test our ability at that which should be impossible. If we fly, why not as high as. If anything, not heeding his father's advice only demonstrates his immaturity, but that is no indication of immaturity's belief in immortality or even sustainability.

Again: we each would fly, because we each know that to stay would mean death—literal, violent, bloody death at the hands of a monster (a literal, violent monster who would break through walls, gnash at us, choke us). Fly, *or else*. Or else Minotaur, or else starvation, or else. Fly or else no flight. Altitude, here, like time and light-years, is only another way of measuring distance.

Daedalus's expectation of Icarus's overzealous flight may prove either protective or destructive. His advice was given knowing this boy's (any boy's—anybody's) tendency to extremes, but the wax would only suffer if he went too high.

The lower feathers were attached with wax (and where, indeed, did Daedalus find so much (of wax or so many feathers) inside his labyrinth, unless the whole structure was designed to produce or gather these in protective anticipation of incarceration), while those eight primaries were attached with string.

When I consider the feathers used, the immediate image is of seagull feathers, given the amount of water, given the island and the latitude. The association, then, is with the M-wing, militaristic, like the seagull's. And while this is probable, I also consider the number of corpses littering the labyrinth left by the Minotaur; I decide that carrion feathers would be just as probable as seagulls': just as Icarus swung his arms around to feel the rush of blood to his fingertips, so too would the ravens or the vultures circle in the air above.

Seagull wings are perhaps the most easily collectively imagined, because they are white and gray, the way we imagine angels' wings to be, and sleek and smooth the way we imagine humans to be; but they are small in comparison to a vulture's, and we would need the largest feathers possible to fly in myth— mythically large feathers (more likely those of a roc). I think that for efficacy, the primaries would need to be these flat dull muted black vulture feathers, although I do enjoy the image of a mix: pairing these with alulae and secondaries fashioned from seagulls'. This would create what I imagine to be a balanced and beautiful wing—dynamic and strong, long and thick.

Regardless.

Daedalus's design attached the feathers that are principally used to gain *thrust* more securely—using a method of attachment that would less easily succumb to the heat, to the sun—while the feathers designed (necessary) for *lift* were attached with wax, the very downfall of the design.

The man was a genius (Minos knew it), and he is described this way (it is in his name, after all), as so *cunning* as to almost outwit even himself. It should go without saying that someone so intelligent should be able to craft wings. His supplies would have been limited, of course (or perhaps not, by his own design), being trapped in a labyrinth, but the fact with which we are presented is that he had more than just wax at his disposal. And yet, he chose a material that could melt, knowing that there was a serious probability that Icarus would fly, if not too close to the water, too high—*too close to the sun*. This must have been a conscious choice, but the purpose is ambivalent.

Attaching the secondaries with wax could have been a measure to prevent Icarus from flying too high to begin with: reach a certain altitude, and the secondaries would have slid off, preventing him from gaining excess height. This could be a demonstration of the most profound intimacy and knowledge with and of his son, a recognition that his word would not be heeded. Wax, then, could be proof that Daedalus did not want Icarus to soar too high. Destruction, a measure of protection.

But it could also have been sabotage. Again, knowing that Icarus *would* climb to extreme heights, the melting (meltable) wax would, again, prevent him from proceeding higher still;

but so too would it have prevented him from recovering from the fall. Falling, unable to right himself, unable to gain height once fallen. Fallen, indefinitely grounded; fallen, flightless. Also (necessarily) dead.

Although this can't be quite right either: not all of the feathers were lost, so Icarus could have, if not gained height enough to continue flight at a reasonable altitude, then glided, floated, slowly descended in a controlled enough manner to land without crash. I imagine that his immaturity led to significant panic and an inadequate ability to problem-solve: he may simply have not realized that this was a possibility.

Or perhaps he did, and the best he could do was land in the middle of the sea, tied up by his father in his father's heavy wooden flying apparatus, making swimming an impossibility. And slowly succumbing to torrents.

This is so often how it happens, isn't it: we commit to something so adamantly, with so much zeal that we make ourselves see it through, even to the destructive end. Because the alternative is *or else*. We say we will see how far we can go, how long we can sustain it, and then we don't—don't go, don't sustain. And the fall takes only a fraction of the time it took to ascend.

It is the proverbial *crash and burn*, only without the crash, and probably without the burn. Instead, just the flames, the phlogiston, the four pounds of ashes (if there were even one). This is the *emotional* fall from that height.

And it is not just seen in father-son relationships: this obviously trespasses upon many kinds. Once we learn to fly—once we are given the opportunity and tools to fly, we do, because we have never felt so weightless, and we have never felt so free. We test the relationship: how much may I pull back; how close may I get. But there is a definite beauty—a light, a fire—to which we fly, continuously, if circuitously. The warmth of the sun rejuvenates us from a lonely solitude, suddenly, as if we have been trapped outside of it for a very long time. And perhaps we do not yet know how to take things in moderation. And we only have two choices, anyway: get closer to the object that makes us feel as if we are flying (we are, we do), or let ourselves drop unnoticed into the ocean. So the choice is made, because none of us are self-destructive—not admittedly—and we get closer and closer until the pleasant, encompassing heat of that object is the same that engulfs our wings, burns our backs, and we fall without notice. Regardless.

As we swallow our salts and return the water's slaps to stave off the inevitable drowning, we understand that our proximity to the object which guided our flight was destructive. The object—the sun, the romantic other—was not destructive, not innately; our fathers' wax was not inadequate; we possessed both the strength and the endurance; and we each were able to fight gravity well enough to see it through. But we ascend, and the relationship intensifies exponentially—till it elevates to a place we can't breathe. As our face (collective, here) returns to a regular pallor and our carotid arteries deliver oxygen again and our swollen supratrochlear artery inters itself under our blackened, flaked skin—there is nothing left to grieve, because we have that for which we (perhaps) flew: the damage that proves we did—we flew higher, and we survived.

My skin continues to peel, only now in small holes near my wrists, like blisters, like open pustules, like cavities that I open wider and carve deeper. I know that this is new damaged skin being exposed and sloughed as quickly; I know that this could also be bits of flesh that were not damaged as severely and are thus rejected less quickly (as if they have been still remotely recognizable and usable). I associate this, though, with the knowledge that our skin continues to burn even once we remove it from ultraviolet exposure. We cook from the inside out. And these flaky eruptions, almost insignificant when compared to my scabbed and desiccated shoulders, seem that way to me: my bones provide the heat, and my skin is now at a rolling boil.

And my therapist asks what would happen if I did not intellectualize these experiences: if not, then my skin *is* boiling from a heat that must exist somewhere inside me. And Icarus *did* fly and flew high and crashed and died. And there is nothing to explain the ribbons of flesh falling from my shoulders. And the pictures are as, if not more, accurate: his wings *were* his own, and they grew from his back, and when they burnt, it was terrible; the bones became exposed, charred there too, crumbled to just the frame—just ulna, metacarpus, phalanx. If I did not intellectualize the burn or the time between us, then that time would not exist, and the burn would be much more frightening, because it would be unexplained. Memory would contract everything, and he would be very close, still, and our fingers would overlap over my own shoulders, pulling some of the same flesh off of me—never having grown or shed or changed or burnt again. My skin would tell me that something has changed, but nothing hurts. And that would be it. If, then it is all conflated and impossible.

The physics of all this is a way to manage the site of trauma, keep it as clean as possible so that it may heal without scarring, to tidy it up to prepare for something else: the definite answers to the definite, serious problems, the math involved, the narrative itself, the fantastic images that I can't not see now—they give me something to say, words to speak into what is otherwise an absence, a reason for or cause of the damage I (again) find (on (*in*) me).

The fall could not have surprised him. (I wonder if falls ever do.) To climb to such ecstatic heights, we may only plummet. And he would have exhausted himself, buffeting his wings so vigorously and adamantly to, perhaps, make up for such flimsy feathers. How often do we find ourselves tired from attempting that which we know we should not be able to do—continue the ascent when all we want is to glide, for things to be easy. That is part of the (romantic) commitment: try as we may, we get as far as we can, and when we cannot proceed further, we cannot proceed further. So end.

For Icarus, there would be that moment of stillness at the full height when his momentum waned as gravity dominated again (as if it ever doesn't). Just a singular moment of weightlessness— between (merging) ascent and descent—before falling for mere seconds before what I imagine as an eruption into the flames he and his wings would become. And I wonder how long that singular moment feels: to look up and see, unimpeded by atmosphere, all the stars and see below the aurora and past that to the earth that has become unrecognizable and, suddenly, spherical.

Does that stretch the moment. And if so, how long does it seem. Do we stretch a singular moment into years—or three. And when it is over, do we remember the years, or does it contract back into negligence—our backs a clayey landscape of mud cracks.

Eve

Teach me to bury this. Teach me to rub lemons over all this. How do I nip a thing in the bud, kill at the root. How do I cross a puddle that lay so cadaverous and awful or enter a room when so many are watching.

A dead raven. Surprising to see how limp: I know we loosen when we vacate our bodies, but we bloat, and we stiffen. I know this, but birds seem different: no part of them seems soft even in life, nothing comforting, nothing to stroke, nothing to eat except too-hard muscle. They are so many feathers and not much else. I want to touch it, because I have held a dead animal before, and there is something about the rolling head that is both pleasing and terrible.

This is spectacle. And thousands of ravens come to see it, though not all at once. Some better fight the urge than others, slowly materializing. They arrive in threes or twos or sometimes fewer. As the faces slowly appear, it becomes more obvious that they are all dumb faces, without thought or expression. Dumb faces all pointing in the same direction, encompassing. There is a visual threshold, so they are only so far away, but very far away: a match at a mile. They keep appearing, though, so they encroach on our space. To see you. And there is a limit, and it creates a border just out of my reach, just beyond my outstretched knuckled finger and oval nail. I dream of nothing but boundaries and dreams between my breasts.

One of these visiting ravens comes closer. It scratches at the dry yellow ground, now collecting under its nails, and isn't it amazing how something yellow seems so brown under keratin and hair. And it scratches for a very long time. Change is always so slow. I am mourning you, weeping. My forehead is dustily transparent, rasp, and my cheeks are dirty the way lips get dirty and then peel, the way we peel back plastic wrap, and the way we only clean that which we can reach.

I pause and wonder momentarily at who has sent this raven, why this raven acted differently than the rest. I trust it was god, though I have been foolish about snakes before.

The yellow ground is so dry, and it flakes, coming up in plaster chunks, but the residue only falls into the newfound absences, the air pockets, and leave a layer of something porous, covered and pressed, stamped, with something fine. Scratch, but it is like wax on unfinished wood, like something thin on something flat, and no nails can get under it. It breaks and chips and smashes and dusts finer and finer, until all that the raven can do is take its tiny head, point his beak into its chest, and push it all away, leaving its forehead and cere matted with ground or ash. And then all it can do is somehow begin again. Another thin layer.

The raven looks frantic, rushing. This must be done by May, but this is so difficult. There is grease and dust covering everything, and each hour of work only changes so little.

How can you be at this for so long. Are you really digging for five or six or ten hours at a time. I can't imagine anything to be this difficult. I can't imagine.

He can't imagine. But it *is* this difficult.

Until finally it is not, and enough layers have been scratched away, built up like a crater, piled about like stones, like ravens viewing carrion. Until finally the only remaining task is to push the thing, the dead raven, into this shallow hole. The raven pushes the dead raven, the thing, into this shallow hole and then turns around and faces me in some horrible way with exhausted eyes with sagging skin and brow and bloodshot and so fucking dark, so beautifully dark. I watch as it uses its wings to flap back all that yellowed dust.

Only now, with the thing covered, do I understand: the raven has shown me what to do with this burst appendix, you, this body—this first lifeless body. The raven is frantic and rushing, yes, because the raven is insistent: it would be awful to not do this; it would be awful to leave this incomplete; it would be a bad thing to do anything but this, even though there are so many other things to do. You have to bury, but I am so tired.

I protest. I don't want your hard lines covered this way. I don't understand this, this death, this lifelessness or this just-body. But I know that this raven is telling me what must be done for my kin who has fallen the way I have felled so many of his creatures. Unfit for food. And loved. But I don't want him to tell me what to do with a dead body; I want him to make the lifeless body not a dead body.

If you can send a message, you can revive the dead. So then why not.

I don't want you covered, because I am not ashamed of you, I should not be ashamed of you, the way I am of my own body. But yours is a body too, so of course I am ashamed, that is why I am here, on the ground, covered in dust, weeping; and that is why he came and told me what to do with you. But I knew once that there is nothing shameful in a body to hide. If shame exists in your flesh, I implanted it in you, the way he placed the seed of it in mine. I projected it. So the question is not whether you need to be hidden. The question is, *Am I ashamed of you.*

Yes.

But this shame is mine, not yours, never because of you, but because I am ashamed of my narrow back and wide hips, of my inability to distinguish between emotions and sex, of my ears and teeth, and of my inability to rightly exist in my body the way you once did yours. I am ashamed that there is nothing thrashing in me, that I am making no attempts at anything other than at attempts. I try to try, but you do. And I am ashamed of you, yes, in part. So he came, the raven did, and he said, *Bury it. Cover it.*

And I could end it that easily. But the problem is not how to measure difficulty. The problem is a question: *Do I want it ended.*

No.

I will never be done with you, I think. I can't say I am just beginning with you, because everyone says that, and I want to be first, best, more than enough. Good enough. I want to be able to say that I could put you away at any moment.

Abel keeps secrets, hidden with him under this yellow ground. Cain is the storyteller, so once I told him, the world knew. Now we know to bury a raven. Now we know how we know to bury the dead, if we *do* bury the dead. And I am always before the story.

Through phone-cans and aging voices, the same story becomes the suggestion that it is bad luck to kill a raven. As if burial demonstrates attrition. As if a corpse alone is proof of violence. And I admit, this *is* violent. But it isn't bad luck to kill anything.

You can drown anything. But the corpse is yours to do something with. So we bury to hide our shame with it.

I've wept at not knowing what to do with you. Nothing exists as an appendix, grown useless and fit only to burst. Nothing is a placeholder, but rather is singly, wholly loved. And when I am sad, I am vacant. Just this body. My eyes still see, so I look straight ahead because all my muscles are stiff cement. Nothing but barren landscape, just a path, just your body, lying in the road. The entire world becomes just my body and your body. Without lodgment. We could be anywhere: Eden, Egypt, Chicago. Against the lake, in the mountains, on the rocks.

How do I still have all my fingernails. And how do you. I break one off and throw it to the ocean, and I consider the waves of blood. This throbbing digit is for you. The uncracking knuckles and blistered shoulders, this burnt hair around my right wrist, this scar, here—all for you.

I am frustrated. I weep, like this. I throw myself amongst shredded papers on the floor, and I forget that you are somewhere, watching me. And you are embarrassed at my inability, calling away those who might see; attracting everyone, giving priority to *your* ability so that none is given to the possibility that I might fuck up.

In a frenzy, I shove the snow aside so that I can do this for you, so that I can give you this one message. I lift and carry something too heavy for my frame, and I launch it to the ground in the hope of making a crater to end Russia and you with it.

But I feel immobilized, any of my attempts at attempting, futile: for as much shit and ejecta and debris there may be, the compression wave has only compacted that which I must till. I create for myself an impossible density that cannot be pushed aside.

So how much of this will linger, decay here in the air. How many times have I given myself something to bury without the strength to dig. I have gone through sixteen, now seventeen ways now of telling you one thing only to find that there is no way of telling you at all. I can only hope you come to find me in a dark, damp, wide-mouthed cave a thousand ages from now and I have the strength to lift my limp wrists to present you with my broken nails and rough hands, to point and show you that that, there, is what I tried to make for you.

Notes

The title "I thought it would happen as in a myth." comes from Deborah Tall's *A Family of Strangers*, and the title "No-One Suspects Your Shoulder Blades of Wings" comes from Jeanette Winterson's *Written on the Body*.

"Mother" (82) was the first of these essays begun as well as one of the last to be finished—the most difficult because the content was the most frightening: not only literary forebears, not only illness and the body, but also creativity and writing and writing illness and writing the body. Woolf inspires just as she intimidates, so the only way I could get myself to utter it completely, if imperfectly, was by using a soliloquy from one of her last novels, *The Waves*. The words, spoken by the character Rhoda, were appended with quotes from Woolf's essay "On Being Ill" and supplemented by my own rumination and speculation.

March 2016
Chicago, IL

Biographical Note

Wes Jamison is the author of the chapbook *and Melancholia* (Essay Press, 2016) and is a noted author in *Best American Essays*. They earned an MFA in nonfiction from Columbia College Chicago and a PhD in English from the University of Louisiana at Lafayette. They currently teach at Del Mar College in Corpus Christi, Texas.

Printed in the USA
CPSIA information can be obtained
at www.ICGtesting.com
JSHW080053060424
60628JS00002B/4